The New Road to
Successful Advertising

The New Road to Successful Advertising

How to Integrate Image and Response

Carol Nelson

Bonus Books, Inc., Chicago

95 94 93 92 91   5 4 3 2 1

Library of Congress Catalog Card Number: 91–72705

International Standard Book Number: 0-929387-53-8

Bonus Books, Inc.
160 East Illinois Street
Chicago, Illinois 60611

First Edition

Printed in the United States of America

This is dedicated to Herschell Gordon Lewis. Thanks, Hersch, for being my unwavering ally, my good friend—and my best critic.

Contents

Foreword

This book is not for everyone. It will challenge the hard-liners in both the world of advertising and direct marketing. It will upset those who believe these are two different worlds, separated by a viewpoint that advertising only creates images, and direct only sells.

For the open-minded reader, it will shed new light and insights into a far more important issue, the Dawn of Integrated Communications; and provide the understanding required to make use of the range of communication disciplines in an increasingly cluttered world.

Over sixty years ago, John Caples wrote brilliant and creatively intrusive copy for a range of products and services, consumed only with a single passion: how to best communicate with customers and motivate them to act.

In the intervening years, with the development of new forms of communication and phrases like direct marketing and sales promotion, and new media forms from television to video disks, the focus shifted from effective communication to techniques and sometimes even tricks.

The consumer was forgotten, relegated to an audience who some hoped would react and respond to new forms of gadgetry. Some advertising and marketing people forgot that to the consumer, regardless of what practitioners called it, it was ALL advertising. And even if its purpose was tactical to bring about a response to a compelling offer, an impression was made. Sometimes good, sometimes less positive. And it was, and remains, relevant images and copy which produce response in any form.

The New Road to Successful Advertising provides a clean and fresh roadmap to what truly relevant communication is about. It presents a New Age of advertising, when all advertising must do double duty. When thinking only of here and now and the response rate will be thought of as only one element in successful direct marketing. And when all advertising must be more carefully targeted to reach and communicate to a changing marketplace...building brand equity, yes, but producing meaningful results in a measurable fashion as well.

John O'Toole, former Chairman of Foote, Cone & Belding, and now President of American Association of Advertising Agencies, said about the future of the advertising landscape: "Advertising must be redefined to comprise all marketing communication direct to the consumer. The future belongs to those agencies that can truly integrate these services."

The second part of this book is equally controversial. It will upset writers who believe form is more important than content. For others, who recognize that a contemporary consumer will no longer be motivated into action—direct or at retail—without reaching them where they live.

The time-starved consumer with an increasingly complex lifestyle, suffering from sensory overload, will not spend time with uninteresting advertising in any form. "Interesting" takes on a new meaning: Not simply artfully created images presented in mind warping speed, but advertising which combines a gift for sight, sound, and words with an equally centered understanding of the consumer.

For those who think the future will be a drab place devoid of creative opportunities, Carol Nelson brings you hope. A new horizon of electronic media will be part of your creative palette. What those final forms will be? How large they become, is not yet known. What is known is they are here to stay. Just as desktop publishing has become a reality, so will some of the new technologies.

These new media will present new creative challenges. No less a challenge than when copywriters of the 1950s were asked to adapt their skills from four-color bleed pages in *LOOK* magazine to something called television. To go from hundreds of words to a handful. These new challenges will be greater. To create new advertising in such forms as computer disks, or video text screens on computer monitors with and without sound, will require a new form of creativity: direct interactivity. It will communicate one-on-one.

Unless the originators of this advertising harness an understanding of this extraordinary opportunity to speak with you and me as individuals they expose themselves to terrible risk. The obvious one is a feeling that your privacy and mine has been invaded for no good reason. If these new media are simply used to deliver mass messaging, the word ''irrelevant'' will take on new meaning. Worse yet, if the communication to me in my home or office is not seen as relevant, the greater risk is simply to be ignored.

You will find this book an enlightened view of a new world of advertising ...bringing together disciplines once separated by media, technique and turf...showing the way for a new generation of advertising and marketing professionals to understand that their future lies in developing enhanced skills across all communication disciplines.

''...Leave the dreams of yesterday, take the torch of knowledge and build the dreams of the future.'' (Marie Curie, on the twenty-fifth anniversary of the discovery of Radium.)

Jerry I. Reitman
Executive Vice President
Leo Burnett Company—Chicago

Preface

Relevance.

Relevance. It's *the* fashionable buzzword of this decade.

What does "relevance" mean—in advertising?

This: If our customers don't understand—and understand up front—exactly how our product and our sales message are relevant to them, they're going to turn the page . . . throw away the letter . . . flip the dial . . . or, as far as we're concerned, move to Mars (where, at least in this decade, they won't be annoyed by *ir*relevant advertising).

We're wallowing in the "information glut" of the 1990s.

Glutted as we are, overloaded as our senses are, as "burned out" professionally as we feel at the end of each message-assaulting day, how many of us consciously take the time to assimilate and review even the routine options we have just to get every day started? Before we even begin to transmit messages of our own (adding to other people's glut!), we're exhausted from reading the morning news, figuring out which suit to wear, wondering whether an egg will overload our cholesterol-infested arteries, and deciding which crowded freeway route will get us to the office in less time than it did yesterday.

That's one of the barriers we who practice the "profession" of advertising have to crash through: Daily routine.

How do we do that?

We make each and every piece of advertising we write relevant to the person receiving our message.

We make it our business to know *exactly* whom we're writing to. Who they are, where they live, what they buy. And why.

Knowing all this gives us the ammunition to write persuasive sales messages. Our targets will respond to persuasion; they won't respond to bluster, our self-interests, or rhetorical arrows shot randomly into the air.

You say you're a copywriter? Or maybe you have copywriters working for you? Okay, on a scale from 1 to 100, how effective is your writing in the 1990s?

The professional advertising copywriter who wants to survive in the brutal 1990s not only has to understand both basic advertising and direct marketing, but how to use both to convert a prospect into a customer.

This means more than learning new "rules." It means using new rules to leap beyond *technique*—which a reasonably bright student can master—into creative salesmanship—which is what professionalism is all about.

Some writers decide to become *copy*writers. They know colorful words and poetic phrases. And their copy may get up to 50 on that scale of effectiveness, if they're lucky. But a copywriter had better hit at least 90 time after time.

The difference between writing and copywriting: Our words have to hit and penetrate a target, or we've wasted money. We're not poets; we're *persuaders*.

I have two jobs to accomplish with this book. My first job is to sort out the differences between "conventional" (image) advertising and hard-boiled direct marketing. Then I'll explain why those of us who call ourselves advertising professionals had better master the technique of *integrating* the two, and master it fast.

My second job is to explain how those who write for the information-glutted 1990s reader, viewer, or listener can become stronger persuaders.

Your logical question is, "How is she going to do that?"

First, by showing you some of the newer techniques and technology you may not have seen. . .techniques and technology designed to help increase your writing's pulling power.

Second, by tying together the components of successful integrated advertising. To understand how to write targeted copy, we have to understand media and list selection. We have to understand art direction. We have to understand general advertising as well as direct response. And we *always* have to be on top of what's new and changing in print formats.

Third, by showing you examples of ways advertisers have succeeded (and failed) in cutting through the clutter. You not only can draw your own conclusions; you'll have samples to use for comparison when you write.

Let's repeat and repeat our basic litany: A successful copywriter is a successful *marketer.*

We can't truly call ourselves successful advertising people unless we identify ourselves as marketing people. That's the difference between mere writers and copywriters. And that's the difference we'll explore.

CHAPTER *1*

Improved Image and Improved Response: The Impossible Dream?

Are we entering a brave new world of advertising?

Direct response, a term unheard of twenty years ago and ignored by *Advertising Age* and its subscribers until just a few years ago, is no longer a separate category of advertising and sales promotion.

Advertising agencies are gobbling up direct marketing agencies and specialists in order to continue their claims of being "full service" agencies.

We're witnessing marriage after marriage of traditional image-driven advertising and hard-boiled direct response. Not only aren't these marriages ending in a divorce; the parvenu, direct marketing, has become the head of the family. A 1990 study of advertising budgets by *Business Marketing* showed a total of 94 billion media dollars spent. Of these, $8.6 billion went to general advertising; $30.1 billion went to direct marketing (of which an astounding $27 billion was attributed to telemarketing).

Whether we believe these figures or not, we can't ignore the overtones: Direct marketing has become a full partner, and the key question of the 1990s isn't, "Should we include direct marketing in our campaign?" but "How do we . . . ?"

Is Image Passé?

Does corporate image suffer when direct response enters the marketing picture? Or is image passé in today's brutally competitive marketplace?

The era of advertisers trying to outdo each other with empty splash and mechanical tricks has to end soon. It's as close to obsolescence as the name "Twentieth Century Fox."

Why? Because direct marketing has educated clients *and* the public to what advertising *should* do.

> In the final decade of the twentieth century, we find ourselves in a communications glut. The result of any glut—whether it be product, service, or communications—is apathy. Our job as communicators is to adapt our own techniques to combat this new apathy.

Apathy. This latter-day communications pest is like a nest of cockroaches. We'll never wipe out the colony, but we sure can spray it with our new communications-insecticide: a potent formula mixed from direct and image marketing. Leave out one ingredient and the mixture won't foam.

Within this very decade, our automatic rhetorical spray-machines should be in place. Let's take an early look at methods advertisers can use to improve response in the face of increased competition and decreased recipient interest.

Facing the New Age

Advertising faces a new age of sophistication: Our targets, whether business or consumer, have been *desensitized* to traditional sales communication.

If we as professional communicators don't combat this apathy, we gradually lose our ability to convince neutral or skeptical message-recipients of two points: 1) Our own sincerity (a necessity for building rapport); 2) The validity of our offer (which our best targets have trained themselves to reject).

"General advertising" goes under a few names. Some call it "image advertising," some call it "conventional advertising." (You'll see all three terms in this book used interchangeably.) By whatever name you choose to use, general advertising usually refers to broadcast and print.

Its main purpose is *getting attention.*

Many writers of general advertising concentrate on setting a mood rather than selling a product. A lot of advertising exists to create an experience, or a thing of beauty.

These are admirable goals in advertising—but they're not *the* primary goals of advertising. The primary goal of advertising is to sell a product or service; and successful general advertising creates a mood, an experience, a thing of beauty, combined with product benefits—to *help sell* that product or service.

But as general advertising turns in on itself, as it creates more and more "moods," more and more "experiences," the threat—in some cases, already a reality—is its transformation into advertising for the advertising insiders: advertising (or *non*-advertising, really) whose main purpose is to win awards instead of advertising to create awareness of and sell a product.

For years, advertisers have been satisfied if people just remember their ads. In the 1990s, the question isn't, "Did you remember the ad?" but "Did the ad persuade you to do something you wouldn't have done if you hadn't seen or heard the ad?"

Direct marketing is also known as "direct response advertising." (You'll see both terms in this book used interchangeably.)

The main purpose of direct marketing is *getting a sale.*

Many writers of direct response advertising concentrate on facts rather than setting a mood. A lot of direct response advertising exists as tired formulae and formats with little regard for artistry.

But as direct response turns in on itself, as it relies more and more on the computer and the database, the threat—in some cases, already a reality—is that the creative product, which should be the salesmanship, becomes nothing more than an overused solicitation template plugged into a database hole.

In the realm of this bean-counting mentality, direct response, too, becomes advertising for the database insiders, with little regard for the person who receives the solicitation. That means the only people who are getting an impression from this type of advertising are the ones who actually respond. Worse, it can mean, if non-responders have an impression at all, that impression is one of annoyance.

So direct marketing bears a cross too. Non-responders vanish into limbo, with the only memory of the soliciting company, if any, one of "junk mail."

It doesn't have to be.

Negative Trends of the 1990s

In the 1990s we see two unholy trends.

The first trend is within the business of advertising and marketing. Traditional advertising media are losing ground to other forms of marketing media. Communication budgets—dollars which used to be spent on "traditional" media such as television and print—are being diverted to telemarketing, trade shows, direct response advertising, and sales promotion.

(In addition to the figures on page 1, consider these: American marketers are spending $21 billion on trade shows and more than $7.5 billion on sales promotion. The total is more than three times the total dollars spent on general advertising.)

This isn't necessarily good. It *is* a sign that communication managers are becoming more concerned about the accountability of their advertising and the return on advertising investments.

> Shareholders and top management are looking at the numbers to see where their company has a solid boost of dollars coming in compared with dollars going out. . .and where it hasn't.

The second trend is in the consumer realm. In the environmentally conscious 1990s, activists—and they seem to be breeding like rabbits—have latched onto a "righteous" reason to stop direct mail: the "green" movement. So much mail is discarded, unopened, into the landfills, a grass-roots movement to stop third-class mail delivery altogether is beginning to steamroll.

> Rather than become indignant at the knowledge consumers are throwing out the fruits of hard work, direct mailers should instead take this as a serious signal of the mass irrelevance of sales messages mailed out.

Do these negative trends mean we need advertising re-education? Maybe. More likely, advertising is entering a lean and mean period in which advertising professionals—real advertising professionals who use media to generate real demand—will suddenly be very much in demand.

We're already seeing this. Ask any "headhunter" who specializes in advertising personnel what changes the 1990s have brought, relative to demand for talented practitioners.

Advertising writers and art directors are being asked to do a lot more than just create ads. Successful advertisers now have to be prepared to offer strategic ideas to market a client's product or service. And this development isn't about to disappear. It isn't a fad or a phase; it's the result of recognition that if the cash register doesn't ring, a company—however big it (or its image) may have been in less competitive times—can go out of business.

Creativity + Salesmanship = The Future

Terms as well as attitude are beginning to change. Many bellwether agencies are lumping "advertising" and "direct response" and "sales promotion" into the catchall "marketing services."

Changing terms is superficial; believing a reason actually exists for consolidating the facets of advertising, direct marketing, and sales promotion *is* significant. It spells out the formula for the early twenty-first century: Successful advertising will have to temper imagination and creativity with a large dose of the economic and competitive reality of the 1990s.

I'm personally convinced those imaginative, creative, and *versatile* communicators who can also sell a product will be the advertising professionals in big demand.

If I'm wrong, look me up in the year 2010 and tell me so.

CHAPTER 2

Fusing Direct and General: Best of Both Worlds

Early (1988 and before) attempts at combining image advertising and direct response have resulted in some successes, some failures, and some truly bizarre two-headed monsters.

Think way, way back to the year 1986.

Burger King's "Herb the Nerd" campaign of that seminal year first made me glaringly aware of the difference between "conventional" advertisng copy and direct response copy.

One of the most respected advertising agencies in the world, representing one of the best-known fast food operations, was spending about $40 million on a campaign designed to do—what?

Increase awareness? Maybe, but most prospective customers were already aware of Burger King. Change image? Yes, that glorified nincompoop certainly could change Burger King's image—for the worse. Build sales? How?

> When product is secondary and offer, which any direct marketer would rank number one in importance, is nonexistent, the advertiser is substituting ego for marketing.

Advance your calendar to the year 1990. After four years, Burger King was still trying to figure out what their advertising should be saying. They fired the advertising agency that took over from the "Herb the Nerd" agency with a peculiar "We do it like you'd do it" (so what?) campaign and replaced the second agency with *two* high-powered advertising agencies. The result was: "Sometimes you gotta break the rules." This campaign does break the rules—all advertising rules *I* have ever heard of... and then some. (The most obvious rule it breaks is using oblique non sequiturs to try to sell a product—chapter seven.)

Meanwhile, the typical agency writer of print and television ads revels in creating a "visual experience." The formula: Image + Mood = Success.

Creative Awards versus Actual Response

As a member of the advertising agency community, I'm coldly cognizant of the need to build portfolios and win creative awards. That, sadly, is how we measure personal/professional success.

As a copywriter with blood on my hands from a background in direct marketing, I measure an ad's success, and mine as a writer, by just one yardstick: the response it pulls.

In the 1990s, competition for attention and the consumer's dollar in the marketplace has become nothing short of incredible. An advertising person attempting to write any advertising in this decade (whether that advertising is conventional or direct response) without first immersing himself or herself in both disciplines stands to lose the boss, the client, or (sob!) himself or herself a lot of money.

Why? Because...

> As consumers become more sophisticated, advertising segments them and separates them more and more. Consumers expect advertisers to talk to them individually...or at the very least, within a specific market group. Savvy marketers realize this and already have begun to modify their databases—and their advertisng—to target, if not specific individuals, at least specific markets.

8

What can happen when conventional advertising invades the ranks of direct marketing? Too often the result is obscure ads or purely image-building extravaganzas.

You know why? (Here's where I make some instant enemies.)

Because too many conventional advertisers value the word "recall" over the word "response."

The What and Why of Recall

In the world of conventional advertising "recall" means the number of people who can remember something about the ad within a specified period of time after seeing it.

Understand, please: All the ad has to do to qualify as a success is generate recall, not *action*. It's a totally different way of keeping score from the way direct marketers keep score.

Here's an example: The Christmas holidays give us the perfect opportunity to market bottled spirits. What's easier then sending a gift by picking up the phone and ordering it with your credit card? Think a magazine ad is a good way to do it? I agree. Now, *how* do you do it?

Here's how they did it—and by "they" I mean creative teams who usually work in straight conventional advertising.

Figure 2-1 is page one of a four-page ad. It's a right-hand page, naturally. The headline says, "There are two civilized approaches to holiday shopping. You can hire someone to do it for you..."

Figure 2-2 is the inside spread. The headline says "Or use the Chivas method."

Take another look at the involvement device in Figure 2-2, a die-cut wheel affixed to the sheet. It cost a ton of money. It's clever...the way a cunning but unimaginative creative team thinks in terms of awards instead of selling merchandise.

The idea is for you to spin the wheel to whomever you want to buy a gift for...Dad, the plumber, the boss, the boss's secretary, and other worthies...and it tells you what size bottle to buy. Cute, but it still doesn't give me a motivator for buying it.

Figure 2-3 is the back page of this four-page ad.

Figure 2-4 is a closer look at the only words in all four pages that really tell the reader anything.

Below a single weak nonimperative in the tiniest, barely readable sans serif type is the suggestion, "Visit your local retailer or call 1-800-238-4373 to send a gift of Chivas Regal anywhere in the U.S."

If the reader ever gets to the tiny throwaway line with its oblique suggestion to order the product, will the reader lift the phone and order?

If we've read this far, one more sentence in the same teeny typeface catches our interest. It says, "Ask about our limited edition gift tin."

Figure 2-1

The first page of a four-page holiday ad.

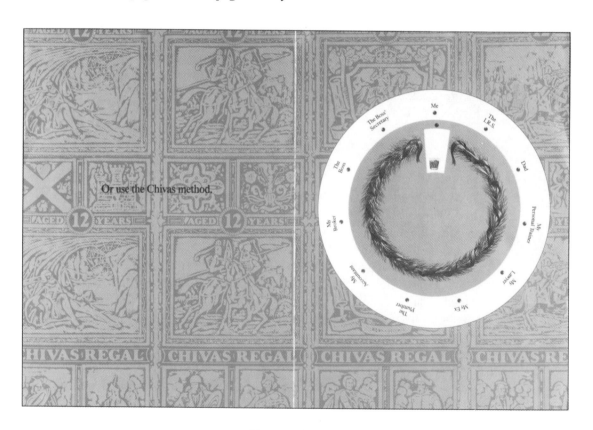

Figure 2-2

The inside spread showing a die-cut wheel affixed to the sheet. It's a clever device, but are high-cost production values a logical substitute for sales motivators?

Figure 2-3

The final page of this four-page ad.

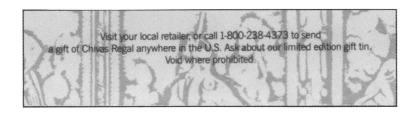

Figure 2-4

A closer look at the buried sales copy—the only copy in all four pages that really tells the reader what to do.

A "limited-edition gift tin"? Isn't that something we might be interested in seeing around holiday gift-giving time? In fact, it might even act as an incentive to read the tiny type. In fact, it might even act as an incentive to buy—if the gift tin were pictured here. In fact, it isn't.

The advertiser's conclusion: Establish our image in the ad and attach a toll-free number. To them—and, I'm afraid, to many of us—adding a toll-free number makes any ad a direct response ad.

I'm curious about one facet of this. It's the quote I read in the advertising trade press from a vice president of the company that distributes this brand of liquor. He said: "We're getting more aggressive in direct marketing. Our direct mail conversion, continuity and telemarketing programs are just the beginning."

The beginning? With such poorly thought-out direct marketing—with an overproduced insert which qualifies itself as direct because it has an 800 number—it could very well be the beginning of the end.

What's missing here is a *motivator*. It's drowned in a sea of production.

Sure it gets attention. But it's the same kind of attention children give to a new toy. A few minutes to figure it out, and then their attention is captured by something else when they turn the page...

And that "something else" grabbing their attention might be the ad in figure 2-5.

It's another ad for bottled spirits—but take a look at the headline. "In this year of perestroika and glasnost, surely you don't plan to give Scotch as a business gift."

This ad, like the ad in figure 2-4, is selling a product for gift-giving. But instead of relying on expensive production to sell, this ad gives the reader a well-thought-out sales argument in favor of not only choosing vodka over scotch, but choosing this particular brand of vodka.

The body copy reads, "Call before December 10th, and we'll guarantee delivery by December 20th. What better way to celebrate the new year and a new world?"

The order phone number is displayed prominently to make the sale while the prospect's buying urge is hot.

An Ancient Rule Still Is Alive and Well

If we're going to teach our counterparts who want to cash in on what we already know, let's repeat an ancient rule of communications that David Ogilvy propounded more then twenty-five years ago:

What you say is more important than how you say it.

That is why the little direct mail company becomes big, despite its originally small budget—and why giant companies waste millions and millions of dollars. The little guys don't have millions and millions to waste. They *know* they have to transmit a motivational message.

Figure 2-5

No big-production/small message in this ad. The copy and art direction work in tandem to present the sales argument. When the reader decides to order, the phone number is easy to find.

Figure 2-6

The first page of a two-page ad loses the reader by burying the sales message in an explosion of disjointed headlines.

> **HOW TO WIN $100,000**
>
> There are two ways to win $100,000: 1) **Instant Winner**–All you have to do is take your High Performance Check to your Valvoline retailer and match your High Performance Check's number with the winning number on the display (See Rule #3). You may have already won $100,000, go find out; 2) **Sweepstakes**–in case your check number doesn't match, you can also enter a drawing for another $100,000. Simply fill out an entry form available at your Valvoline retailer. See rules below for complete details.

Figure 2-7

Page two of the same two-page ad contains the one line that draws in the reader.

Okay, we see what others do wrong. But how about direct marketers? Do they come to the marriage with the proper dowry?

In these times of incredible competition for the consumer's dollars, what can happen when direct marketing invades the ranks of conventional advertising?

Too often we end up trying to compress a direct mail piece into a space ad. The result is something like figure 2.6.

What's wrong with this ad. One *big* thing is wrong.

We have no sales message at all. We have several headlines—Oh, boy, do we have headlines. And they're all competing for attention against one another:

> Oil money.
> It only buys the best.
> And here's a check to prove it!
> And it could be worth $100,000.
> High Performance Check.

Unfortunately, there's no sign of any art direction here, either. I lost count of how many different typefaces coexist in this small space, but using all of them makes this already disjointed ad even more difficult to read.

On the reverse side of this ad in miniature (sans serif) type is *another* headline (figure 2-7)—but this headline draws in the reader better than any of the five different headlines they tried on the front:

> How to win $100,000.

You may think I'm attacking art directors. But I've learned the hard way that a beautiful ad doesn't always sell the product. Even in fashion.

15

Figure 2-8	Figure 2-9

A gorgeous ad—but a beautiful ad doesn't always sell the product. Did the art director and copywriter even talk to each other before they produced this ad?

Another gorgeous ad—but what's the connection between billiards and comfortable shoes?

Figures 2-8 and 2-9 are two shoe ads. They're by the same advertiser, so it's a deliberate campaign. The ads are gorgeous. Beautiful design. Classy use of color (though you can't tell here). The composition in figure 2-8 looks like an interesting painting. The shoe on its side is bright pink and lies in a pile of black lava-like gravel. The headline:

If it feels good. . . Naturalizer.

Wait a minute. Rocks in my shoe aren't my idea of comfort. And a bright green lizard crawling up my ankle makes me cringe, not feel good.

Shoes on a pool table might be a good way to show off the design with color (figure 2-9), but when I read the headline:

Chalk it up to comfort

it seems like too much of a stretch just for wordplay.

On the other hand, the headline in figure 2-10:

> Looks like a pump, feels like a sneaker.

might be just what I'm looking for.

This energetic copy describes how comfortable these shoes are—and why. They even make it easy for me to find the shoes by providing a toll-free number for the store nearest me.

Yet there's not much style in the way they're presented. From what I can see these shoes don't have much panache because the ad wasn't art-directed well.

Much as I want a comfortable pair of shoes, I'm not going out of my way to buy any of these. On one hand, I have beauty without reason, and on the other, reason without beauty.

So How Do We Combine the Two?

So just how can we combine general advertising's style and knack for getting attention with direct's mail's salesmanship in a print ad?

The headline in figure 2-11 reads:

> Before you lay out 1,100 francs for a pair of Louis Vuitton
> gloves, here are a few things to consider. To begin with,
> Louis Vuitton doesn't make gloves.

Media choice for this ad was proper—an upscale city magazine. And what a perfect use of a long headline. You're duped by the ad, as you would have been if you decided to buy the gloves. But it's not unpleasant. Copy forces you to read on to find the other reasons. You get useful information and you're led to believe there's more of it you can use if you buy the product. Which happens to be a travel magazine.

By the time you've read the ad through, you're ready to buy the magazine. But—and this is where they lose you—how do you get it? Well, I guess you'll have to go down to the newsstand to pick it up.

Who knows if you'll make the effort?

If you do go to buy it, again who knows? You might be distracted by the competition's cover. Why not include a way to order the subscription while the buying urge is hot? It would have been so easy for the writer of this ad to move in for the sales kill by adding a toll-free number, a subscription coupon—anything! Why not think like a marketer, as long as you finally have art direction to match the message?

(And I don't think a picture of the magazine down there by the signature line really would have hurt too much, either.)

I'm looking at a full-color, full-bleed ad for a brand of cigarettes, More

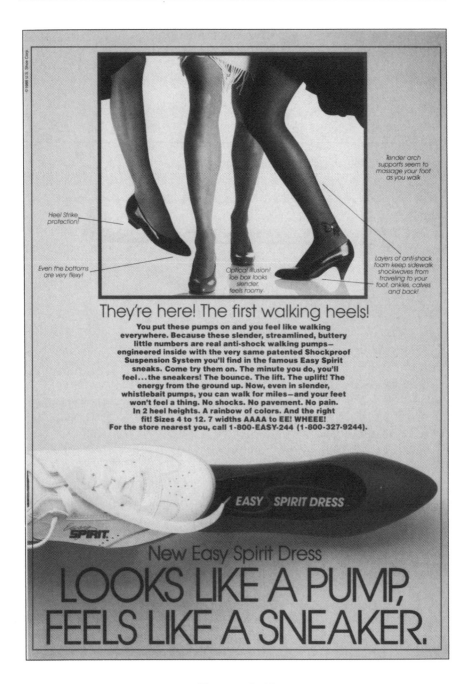

Figure 2-10

Energetic copy here gives us a good motivator to buy—even a toll-free number to find these shoes. But the visual presentation doesn't enhance the style of the product.

Figure 2-11

This engaging copy from the left-hand page of a two-page spread convinces the reader to buy—but how? A subscription order form, address, or phone number would have been effective here.

Figure 2-12

Here's an ad that does—what? It merely *announces*. It doesn't lead the reader, as a direct response ad would do, and it doesn't generate an attitude, as in image ad would.

Figure 2-13

This company demands attention and response with a pop-up coupon.

(see figure 2-12). The entire text of the ad (other than the required legal copy) is:

Dare to be More.

The ad shows a young woman leaning on a huge pack of cigarettes. Its purpose? To establish visibility.

The ad isn't terrible, but at the risk of being branded a heretic I'll opine it was easier to write than a direct mail piece by a local drug store soliciting customers for that same brand. All the ad does is *announce*. Is a mood established? If so, it would differ among various readers because some would say, ''Oh,'' some would say, ''I like her outfit,'' some would say, ''Nice job of art direction,'' and some would say, ''How ridiculous.''

Would *any* reader say, as a result of this heavily-produced ad, I'll go out and buy that brand''? Unlikely. Why? Because it doesn't lead the reader, as any worthwhile direct response ad would do. And it doesn't even try to generate an *attitude*, as an alert image ad would do.

Another ad for a brand of cigarettes went with a four-page bound-in insert with a pop-up. It, too, is heavily produced.

Heavily? Titantically!

But at least this one demands a response with the pop-up coupon (figure 2-13) and the offer of three free packs when you buy two.

These days, the battle for the customer isn't the only fight cigarette companies are engaged in: They're also battling for their right to pay for advertising space. Legislation, which already banned cigarettes from the airwaves in the early 1970s, now threatens to ban them from space advertising and even billboards. What's left for cigarette advertisers? Direct marketing.

The Beginnings of Database Use

Enterprising cigarette companies are pursuing smokers by using space ads to induce smokers to write to them. That way, they capture the smoker's name and build that magical word of 1990s marketing: *Database*.

Figure 2-14 is one from Virginia Slims. It's a contest (involvement value), but the company doesn't take the risk that the reader will get bored with solving the contest and give up without ever entering. No, this company uses its entire copy block to get readers to ask for the rules of

Figure 2-14

Virginia Slims involves the reader with a contest: one way to get the reader to pay attention to your ad. In the meantime, the company collects information—to establish a future relationship with respondents.

These models need dates.

In the 22 years that Virginia Slims has been around, fashions have definitely come a long way. And to celebrate our anniversary, we have a challenge for you. If you're able to match each of these Virginia Slims fashions to the year they first appeared, you'll be eligible to win $22,000 for your own shopping spree. And in addition to over $100,000 worth of other prizes, everyone who enters can request a valuable coupon for Virginia Slims cigarettes.

If you'd like to give it a try, write for clues and an entry form to: Virginia Slims Match-Up Request, P.O. Box 12700, Grand Rapids, MN 58745. Then think back to the days of platform shoes, knickers, and hip huggers. $22,000 might even make the disco look worth remembering.

THE VIRGINIA SLIMS 22nd ANNIVERSARY MATCH-UP.

No purchase necessary. Contest limited to smokers 21 years or older. All entries must be received by 12/31/90.

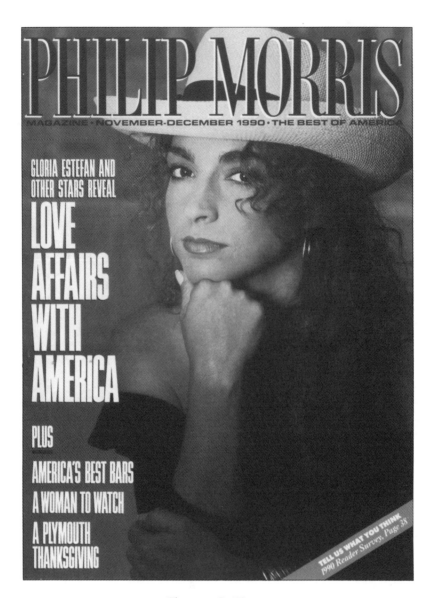

Figure 2-15

Here's one way Philip Morris continues a dialogue with customers: A general-interest magazine mailed to smokers.

the contest, up front. That way, the company has their names (the reason for the contest in the first place) even if they never enter.

How does Virginia Slims use the names? Here's one way: Virginia Slims is a Philip Morris brand. Philip Morris is way ahead of the pack in direct marketing. They've mailed free copies of *Philip Morris* magazine (figure 2-15) for years. Who's a better target than smokers who responded to a Virginia Slims contest?

Philip Morris magazine is a general-interest magazine; but advertisers who buy space know they're reaching smokers.

The magazine carries more than cigarette advertising: You'll find beer advertising, salad dressing advertising—even advertising for rice. That makes sense, of course. Smokers are as good a target audience for packaged goods as the readers of *Good Housekeeping*.

So *Philip Morris* magazine offers a specific group of readers. The magazine *positions* itself. Advertisers who place their ads in this magazine know something about whom they're reaching.

And that's the first key to unlocking the gates that block the integration of general advertising and direct response: Knowing who your customers and prospects are. The next logical step, of course, is aiming your message at those people you've identified.

You've seen commercials where your reaction has been, "Gee, that commercial was really entertaining." And that's good—but can you remember the products those commercials were selling? Did those commercials *reach* you?

Now think of the commercials you've seen when your reaction was, "Hey, I could use that product." You may not remember the commercial, but chances are, the product is now part of your everyday life.

Take a look through the magazines on your desk. Watch the next cluster of television spots. Aren't the ads which present a *convincing* sales argument the ones which point out the benefits of the product to you personally? Aren't they the ones which most resemble direct response ads? They're the siren-songs pulling you to the store or dealership with the downpayment in your fist.

Don't mistake me. I'm not damning all advertising. I love this business and I think communicators are the hope of the future. But in my opinion we should be communicators, not exhibitionists or clever contrivers. Does a message which dances around whatever we're supposed to be selling qualify as a forceful communication?

It depends whom you ask. I've seen copy tossed out before it ever was presented to a client because it was too straightforward. And I've seen clients who sliced vibrant copy down to its own safe and colorless shadow.

As the big agencies (and many medium-sized agencies) start up or buy up direct response agencies, there's bound to be some mixing of the blood.

> Moves toward the center aren't necessarily good. Combining the best of both worlds is.

The answer to my dilemma, and that of other advertising creatives who wonder what drummer they're marching to and who have begun to question the whole concept of "creativity," might be a compromise.

We retain a sense of artistry and flair, one area about which a lot of direct response messages don't seem to care very much. We won't abandon our driving desire to grab attention. What we do is add to our communications-mix a key element we borrow from direct marketing: *persuasive selling arguments*. We refuse to get up from the keyboard until we've satisfied the reader as well as ourselves.

The combination might have two happy results: Recipients won't complain as much about their "junk" mail; and readers and viewers won't score fat zeroes on ad recalls.

Our job—and it isn't "Mission Impossible"—is to grab attention, hold attention, transform attention into a foaming desire to respond, and then shake the reader, viewer, or listener until the envelope is in the mail, the phone rings, or the live body is in the store.

That's what the integrated marketing of the 1990s should generate. That's what this book is about.

Marketing Checklist—Chapter 2

☐ 1. Have you focused your sales argument on what you're selling and given the prospect an offer? Or have you substituted *ego* for *marketing*?

☐ 2. Do you know who your customers and prospects are? Are you aiming your advertising message at them?

☐ 3. Does your ad consider what your intended target wants to know? Or is it obscure or purely image-building?

☐ 4. Does your ad *lead* the reader, or have you merely made a token gesture toward generating response?

☐ 5. Does your space ad present a readable, attractive, "non-frantic" sales argument? Or does it try to compress an entire direct mail piece into a space ad?

☐ 6. Does your ad provide an easy way for the prospect to respond?

☐ 7. Have you pinpointed and emphasized the most *persuasive selling arguments*?

CHAPTER *3*

Mastering the Fusion: A Blueprint

I don't have to tell you, "direct marketing" is the darling buzz-phrase of 1990s marketing plans.

Giant general advertising agencies, which ten years ago never even considered direct marketing, now are scrambling to either acquire direct marketing shops or start their own direct marketing subsidiaries.

But too many advertising agencies who know the term don't know how to make this simple formula work:

Match the right message to the right audience, using the right media.

Simple? It's so simple it's primitive. But as we look at some of the creative output appearing in print or on our TV screens, we wonder why so many advertisers and their agencies ignore it.

Create your sales message for—and aim it at—the largest group of people who have the means and potential desire to spend money for your product or service.

Communications gurus will tell you they don't believe in "formula" advertising—and I'm no different. When you doggedly pursue a formula as you're creating advertising copy and graphics, you end up with a sameness that eventually will lose the attention of the customer you're trying to reach.

Why? Because a lot of other advertisers out there are using the *same* formula. And in our glutted, competitive marketplace, consumers will skip over any advertising that doesn't immediately catch their attention.

You want to solve each marketing problem with a fresh, benefit-oriented creative solution. When your target's reaction is, "Oh, I've seen this before," the impact of your message becomes spongy at best.

Every time you sit down to create an advertising message—any advertising message, whether it's a space ad, a mail piece, or a broadcast commercial—always keep in mind *who* the target of your message is, *what* message they'll respond to, and *which* sales medium is the most efficient to reach them.

Unless you match your message to your market group using the right media, it won't matter whether your copy is long or short. It won't matter if the type is big or small. It won't matter if it's in color or black and white ...because it won't pull as well as it should.

Consider a real estate salesperson sizing up a prospect. If the prospect is interested in gardening, the salesperson will emphasize the potential of the grounds. If the prospect cooks large family dinners, the salesperson will show off the design of the kitchen and the spaciousness of the dining room—because a good salesperson knows how to tailor the sales argument to the specific prospect.

> Salespeople know instinctively how to match the sales message to their targets. We certainly should be able to achieve the same little goal deliberately, in print or on the air. If we can't, we aren't salespeople...and we shouldn't be writing advertising copy.

Finding the best prospects for your product or service—finding out who they are and how they feel about you—gives you a huge head start on your competition. You're aiming at individuals; they're shooting arrows into the air.

Using targeting knowledge to expertly tailor your sales message to those prospects carries the hallmark of a professional copywriter. Copy that doesn't? The writer is, at best, a dilettante (and may not even know it).

The Creative Strategy Brief

What do we ask ourselves as we sit down at the keyboard? We ask: Who are our sales targets? What do they want? How do they live? What do they buy? And why do they buy when they buy?

Below is a "Creative Strategy Brief." I offer this sixteen-point "discipline" not as a strict set of rules but as a generalized set of questions to ask yourself as you're figuring out the solution (or alternative solutions) to a marketing problem.

Creative Strategy Brief

Client:
Product or Service:

1. **Objective:** What do we want to happen as a result of this advertising (direct sales, lead-generation, retail sales offer)?

2. **Description** of product or service: What is it?

3. **Purpose** of product or service: What does it do?
   a. **Features** of product or service
   b. **Benefits** of product or service: What does it do for the customer?
      • What is the primary benefit to the consumer?
      • What are the secondary benefits?

4. **Audience:** Whom are we addressing this advertising to?
   a. What **lists** are we using?
   b. What **publications** are we going into?
   c. What are the **other media possibilities** for this audience?
   d. What do **market research/focus groups** say about the people we want to reach?

- **Behavioral patterns:** Who buys, who uses, how do they buy, how do they use the product, how often? Who influences the purchasing decision? What else would they buy if this product was not available?
- **Attitudes:** Lifestyle characteristics, attitudes towards the product and its competitors, likes/dislikes, and reasons why.
- What one person would be our **typical buyer?**

5. **Offer:** What's the "hook"?

6. **Price:** Is it competitive?

7. Other copy points: (list)

8. What is the **"tone"** of this advertising (fun, sincere, whimsical, dignified, serious)?
   a. What will **motivate** the reader (fear, greed, exclusivity, guilt, anger, peer pressure)?

9. Do we have a **sample** of the product?

10. Are there **testimonials?**

11. Will we be conducting **tests?**

12. Will we be working with an established **brand image?**
    a. Is this image to be incorporated into our advertising?

13. What *must* be included (**legal and logo** requirements)?

14. What **taboos** do we have (what *can't* we say)?

15. Why are we better than the **competition** (and what is our competition doing)?

16. What do we include on the **order form?**

The first question has to be the most obvious, the most necessary, and, to the racing creative brain, the dullest: Objective. Without an objective, we're wanderers. We can't pinpoint a target because we haven't clarified what we're doing in our own mind.

Objective answers the question: What do we want to happen as the result of this advertising?

Simple, isn't it? Oh, no, it isn't.
Objective can assume one of four faces:

1. Immediate sale, by phone or mail;
2. Lead generation for later follow-up;
3. Getting prospective customers into the store for exposure to retail salespeople; and
4. Increased awareness of either our company, what we're selling, or both.

So if what we want to happen is to get that phone to ring and bags of mail to arrive at our premises...or if we want to get names for our salespeople to "work"...or if we want to have a bunch of customers slathering in the early morning, waiting for our store to open...*Objective* becomes the prelude; the overture to the other fifteen points.

If we're after increased awareness, objective is considerably more elusive; it's a philosophical concept on our part and an almost unmeasurable effect on the part of our targets.

That, in essence, is why image advertising, without a defined result, is on the wane (see chapter 6).

Of the other fifteen points, *audience* is significant enough to warrant its own chapter in this book (chapter 4). The only other point warranting exploration is number fifteen, *Why are we better than our competition?* This point requires statesmanship, because even giant companies lean toward bluster instead of target-benefit. The rule is absolute:

> The effectiveness of superiority over competitors is welded to the potential buyer's *perception* of what that superiority will do for him or her.

The sixteen sales points are here as a checklist. If you can answer at least twelve of them, you have enough ammunition to write a workmanlike piece of copy.

See how easy it is?

Back to Our "3-Part Rule"

Match the right message to the right audience, using the right media. What professional could argue with this 3-Part Rule?

A lot of advertising professionals whose concern is with form rather than function, that's who.

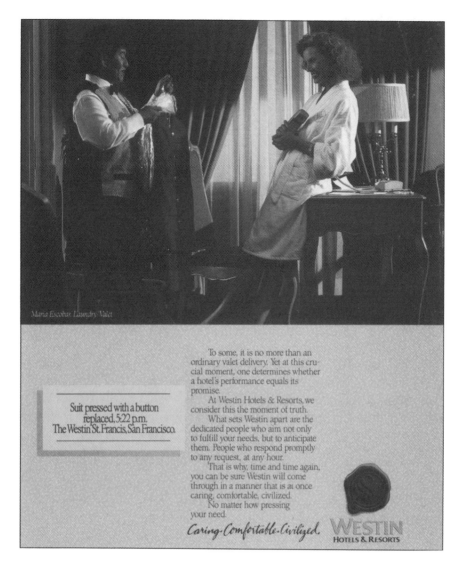

Figure 3-1

This ad ran in a men's fashion magazine. It presents the reader with good, clear benefits for staying at this hotel—but it missed its intended target.

Of course they don't "argue" with it; they just ignore it.

They ignore it out of fear of corporate ego or megalomania, if they're writing for a "personality"-driven company and want to be toadies to the high-profile chief executive.

They ignore it out of sloppiness or laziness if they're not really involved with what they're writing...and *involvement* is as simple and uncomplicated as recognizing that other mini-rule we just read, pointing out the value of buyer-perception.

The ability to generate a ''perception'' is not only as valuable a talent as the ability to invent a product; for a marketer, it can be even more valuable.

Let's look at a couple of space ads created by giant advertising agencies who ignored—in whole or in part—the 3-Part Rule.

Figure 3-1 is an ad for a hotel. The headline reads, ''Suit pressed with a button replaced, 5:22 p.m.''

Good, *clear* competitive benefit for staying at this hotel: immediate valet service when you need it. The photograph shows a woman in her robe, and a valet preparing her suit.

What's wrong with this ad? Nothing. But. . .

Where do you suppose this ad ran? In a general-interest magazine? In a women's business magazine? No, this ad ran in a men's fashion magazine. How many men will identify with this ad?

The marketer who slavishly observes the 3-Part rule would have asked: Why show a woman in this situation and place it in a men's magazine? Wouldn't it be just as easy to substitute a man in the photo? This ad, while it transmits a good and identifiable benefit when placed in a publication aimed at the professional woman, or even in a general-interest magazine, here levels its arrow at the wrong target—the man reading a men's fashion magazine.

What happened? Did the creative department generate one ad, unaware of the media schedule? Believe me, whatever the cause, it wouldn't have happened had this advertiser integrated the media mix into the creative mix.

Figure 3-2 is a space ad selling a car phone. Where do you think it appeared? Not a general business magazine. Not a men's magazine. This ad appeared in a women's business magazine. And what happens when a woman reads it? She has to be jarred by the headline:

> In your position, it's required.

Why? Because the photograph shows a man using the product they're trying to sell.

Why is this ad so jarring? Same reason as the other ad: It misses its target. We aren't being sexist when we suggest logic calls for photographing a man in the hotel ad and a woman in the car phone ad. The magazines where the ads are placed are *vertical magazines*—magazines for a specialized audience.

"You" Had Better Be YOU

The placement problem is made even worse in the car phone ad by the word choice. It's doubly jarring because of the one word that usually makes advertising successful: the use of the word ''you.''

STU III secure cellular.
In your position, it's required.

Figure 3-2

This ad, placed in a women's business magazine, not only missed its target, but compounded the problem by trying to speak personally to the reader. The use of the word "you" can annoy a reader when the message isn't matched to the target.

The word "you" is one of the most powerful words we have in personalizing our advertising to readers. It can make them feel we understand what they want... who they are... and what will make them happy.

Yet "you" is the very word that ruins this ad because the woman reading this business magazine won't bother to read the copy *or* the name of the ad-

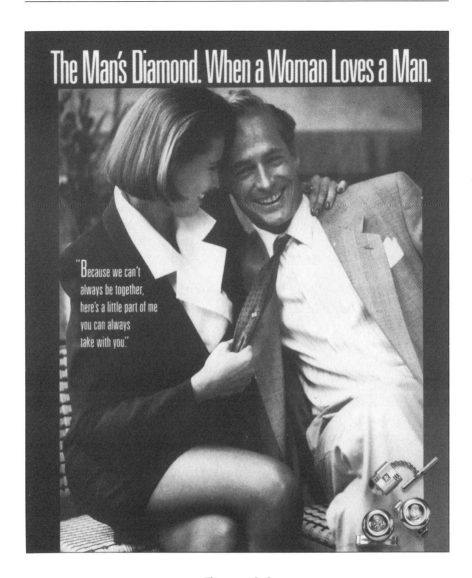

The Man's Diamond. When a Woman Loves a Man.

"Because we can't always be together, here's a little part of me you can always take with you."

Figure 3-3

The use of the word "you" in this ad's headline could have reinforced the targeting—and made the ad more effective.

vertiser in this ad. In fact, if she does read it, and has any reaction at all, it will be one of annoyance.

Whoever made this media decision wasn't professional. Whoever made this decision didn't know or didn't care that as we approach the twenty-first century, we have *segmented* markets. That's the change. That's the evolution we're about to explore. That's the upgrade from the ghost of marketing past: Message, market, medium—all three must match.

Figure 3-3 is an ad that appeared in a men's magazine. How would you change this headline to speak more personally to the target audience?

The Man's Diamond. When a Woman Loves a Man.

If you said you would use the word "you," I give you a star...provided "you" is YOU, the typical reader of a men's magazine, not "you," the giver.

Of course you'd say, "The Man's Diamond. When She Loves You."

Now suppose you want to run the same ad in a women's magazine. What minor change would you make?

You'd say, "...When You Love Him."

See how easy it is. And see how hard it is. It's easy because it's basic targeting. It's hard because you, as marketer, have to become several different people when you write and aim an ad. You have to crawl inside the skin of the person you're trying to reach. You have to know what will motivate someone to buy what you have to sell.

The Natural Evolution of Positioning and Targeting

Let's take a look at how easy it is to target an ad to different audiences when we want to. We "position" the same product to different market groups, within both vertical *and* general interest publications.

Figures 3-4 and 3-5 represent an advertiser who understands the evolution of targeting. These are direct response ads—and they're both selling the same product. It's an exercise machine. In fact, both use the exact same headline—even though they go to two different market groups. Both headlines read:

How to solve the energy crisis.

But what's the difference in targeting here?

One ad was placed in a men's magazine, and the other was placed in a women's magazine. And the correct ad ran in the correct magazine.

Even though the copy is the same in two ads targeted to two separate groups, the ads still work.

Why? Because the company took the time to photograph a man in one and a woman in the other. As a matter of fact, not only did they change models, they changed the tables and chairs, they changed the windows, and they changed the wall paper. They even changed the dogs.

Did they have to change the whole set? No, probably not. In these particular ads, if they'd had a smaller budget to spend, changing the models would probably have been enough, because the placement of these ads—a men's magazine and a women's magazine—is vertical.

Which of these two ads would you use for a general-interest magazine such as *Life, Newsweek,* or *Time?*

Figure 3-4

Nordic Track understands the evolution of targeting. This ad ran in a men's magazine.

Figure 3-5

This ad ran in a women's business magazine. The difference in targeting: The visual was changed to reflect the audience of the magazine.

Either one. A general-interest magazine has no specific audience or gender. If you're a really sophisticated advertiser who wants to know how these specific ads will pull, comparatively, you'd run an A/B split test in a general-interest magazine.

(Just on the wild chance you haven't come across the term before, an A/B split is an even "split" of two ads, printing each ad in alternate copies of the same publication. That means, if you go to the newsstand and pick up two copies of the same magazine, one might have the ad with the man, and the other might have the ad with the woman. It's good way to test two ads to see which one works better. True A/B splits are alternate copies; this assures *demographic equivalence.*)

Now take a look at figure 3-6 to appreciate how this advertiser targeted the advertising to readers of a gourmet food magazine, *Food and Wine*. The headline reads:

> If you've tried eating less
> and still can't lose weight. . .
> something's missing from your diet.

This is especially well-targeted to people who appreciate food so much they subscribe to a magazine devoted to it.

Figure 3-7 is an ad placed in *Longevity*—a publication targeted to readers concerned about health and fitness. The ad is more technical, including charts and graphs. The headline:

> Get weight off and keep it off.

And one last Nordic Track example, figure 3-8, a tongue-in-cheek ad targeted to the readers of *Working Mother:*

> The stress the average mother deals with would bring
> most executives to their knees.

The copy tells us running a major corporation is easy compared with the stress and anxiety caused by the common five-year-old.

Targeting: The Bridge

Targeting is the bridge linking image advertising and direct marketing. Targeting is creating a sales message aimed at *people*. Both disciplines, image advertising and direct marketing, have run off on tangents within the past decade.

General advertisers have fallen all over themselves reaching for the cleverest (or the most beautiful. . .or the most original. . .or the most "creative") way to deliver a sales message. In the competitive crush for

Figure 3-6

This ad ran in *Food and Wine,* a magazine for people who appreciate good food—maybe appreciate it a little too much.

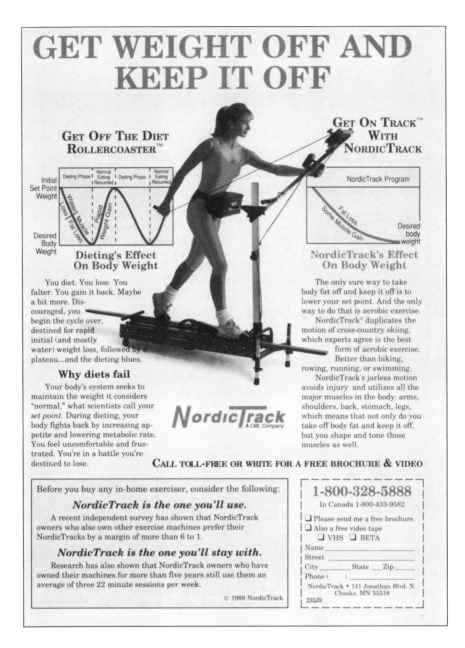

Figure 3-7

This ad, placed in *Longevity* magazine, is targeted to people concerned about health and fitness.

Figure 3-8

This tongue-in-cheek ad speaks personally to the readers of Working Mother magazine.

recognition, too much advertising has aimed at *self*-recognition...and become self-indulgent. So many advertisers seem to have forgotten the reason for the sales message in the first place: To sell a product to *people, not* to produce the biggest, most expensive splash to ever wow judges who pass out awards for advertising creativity. Has "sell" become a dirty word in advertising agencies? A forgotten word?

On the other hand, direct marketers have become so enamored of sophisticated targeting techniques, many seem to have forgotten the word "creative." In fact, some direct marketers treat the word with downright contempt. The mails are overrun with non-messages. Mail packages are aimed at and zeroed in on such perfectly pinpointed, finely-sliced, geo-demo-auto-psycho-gendo-bio-graphic bits of information that many direct marketers have forgotten these bits of information are supposed to translate into *people*.

Have both disciplines hit a 1990s brick wall? Not universally; but the syndrome is widespread enough to present alert marketers with a growth opportunity: Mate the two dinosaurs to create a stronger hybrid.

> Those advertising professionals who recognize opportunity lies in breaking through the brick wall of "we've always done it this way" and in forging new ties between formerly arch-rival disciplines will be the renaissance advertising successes in the coming decades.

. . . Which is the rational conclusion for this chapter.

Marketing Checklist—Chapter 3

☐ 1. Have you created your advertising for the most people who have the means and potential desire to buy what you're selling?

☐ 2. Do you think of yourself as a salesperson while you're writing or laying out the ad?

☐ 3. Have you mapped out your plan of attack by writing a creative brief?

☐ 4. Do you know *whom* your advertising is going to? And are you aiming your sales message specifically to those individuals?

☐ 5. Do you know *where* to place your ad to reach your target most efficiently?

☐ 6. Have you personalized your advertising by liberally sprinkling it with the word "you?"

☐ 7. Are you testing offers and approaches?

CHAPTER *4*

Target Marketing: The Bridge Between Image and Sale

Targeting is the bridge linking image advertising and direct marketing.

Targeting is creating a sales message aimed at specific targets—people.

Target marketing. Everybody in our business loves those two words. But do we really know what they mean?

Let's explore how we as marketing professionals can increase our sales by *targeting*...tailoring our sales message to segmented markets.

Not What We Want to Show, What They Want to See

Too many marketers try to sell us a *method* instead of the *results* of that method. For example, a company sells polybags as replacements for carrier envelopes. They tell us polybags increase visual impact—which they usually do—and then they tell us polybags increase response—which they may or may not do.

Another company specializes in personalization. They'll put an individual's name all over a catalog. It's on the cover, it's on the order form, it's on six different pages inside the catalog. It's on a wrapper around the catalog. It's in four different sizes. The person who gets that catalog drowns in his or her own name.

But while we're admiring this technical tour-de-force, do we think of asking: Did it pull? And if it did, did it pull *enough* to justify the extra cost?

Take a look at two examples. Figures 4-1 and 4-2 are the envelope and contents of one mailing; Figures 4-3 and 4-4 are the envelope and contents of another. Both are brilliant, technically. But one is simply an excellent use of printing technology, while the other is an excellent adaptation of that technology to *reach* the specific individual.

Through the windows of the envelope shown in Figure 4-1 we see computer personalization. If this were the 1970s, the technology would be enough. It isn't. We're well into the 1990s. So when we open this envelope—and we do, because we always open envelopes that offer us something for nothing—we admire all those sizes and typefaces and numbers (figure 4-2). And so we should. The mailing is a technological triumph. But it's a *targeting* weakling, because message is subordinate to technique.

At first glance, Figure 4-3 seems to be the same kind of mailing. It's a sweepstakes . . . and it's loaded with personalization. As you can see from its contents (Figure 4-4), technically it can't compete with the other mailing. But it certainly *can* compete in its ability to *reach its target*.

Look at the copy in Figure 4-3. Somehow this mailer learned that this person goes fishing at Lake Mathews. So this mailing doesn't just use technology for the sake of using technology. It uses technology to connect with this specific individual to whom it was mailed. And *that* is the key to target marketing in the 1990s.

The key to targeting isn't printing the mail recipient's name all over a mail piece. The key to the targeting I'm talking about is that phrase *connect with*. The post office knows how (or *should* know how) to deliver mail. Our job is knowing how to motivate the person whose name is on the envelope.

We're marketers. Our success in the 1990s will depend more and more on our ability to break through the clutter created by other people's advertising.

If you return the grand-prize winning number, our list of prize winners and their guaranteed winnings will be as follows:

ROCKY JAMES ZITZOW
LOS ANGELES, CA
MILLION DOLLAR WINNER!

MINNIE REBECCA HOOD
LAKE ARIEL, PA
MILLION DOLLAR WINNER!

THEODORE SIMPSON
SAN DIEGO, CA
$50,000.00 WINNER!

GEORGE LAWSON
OAK PARK, IL
$25,000.00 WINNER!

01901   CAR-RT SORT **CR·
ROCKY JAMES ZITZOW

If one of the enclosed numbers is returned as Grand Prize Winner, we'll say:

ONE MILLION DOLLARS

FREE GIFT

EARLYBIRD BONUS
Return before
AUG. 5

"ROCKY JAMES ZITZOW, CONGRATULATIONS! YOU'RE ATOP OF THE WINNERS LIST. YOU'LL BE RECEIVING ONE MILLION DOLLARS!"

Dear Rocky James Zitzow,

Thousands of winners have already claimed their prizes in previous sweepstakes presented by SPORTS ILLUSTRATED. The $10,000.00 WINNERS are Joe Dunn of Boise, Idaho, Victoria Garcia of Santa Paula, California, and Frank D. Musgrave of Toledo, Ohio. $25,000.00 PRIZE WINNERS are Rosemary Cooper of Middlepoint, Ohio and George Lawson of Oak Park, Illinois. The $50,000.00 PRIZE WINNER is Theodore Simpson of San Diego, California.

MR. ROCKY ZITZOW, DON'T MAKE US GIVE "THE ZITZOW MILLION" TO SOMEONE ELSE!

Remember, Rocky James Zitzow. You could win the $1,000,000.00 grand prize, and you may also be the winner of a fabulous extra Early Bird Bonus Prize if you hurry and return your entry. To discover the SURPRISE EARLY BIRD BONUS PRIZE you could win, use the edge of a coin to scratch off the GOLD BAR at left. Then be sure to affix the dated Early Bird Bonus Prize Seal to the Entry/Subscription Certificate and return it before AUGUST 5, 1990!

Figures 4-1 and 4-2

A mailing which uses the latest in computer personalization to address the recipient. Does it reach the reader? My opinion: Not as effectively as it could. The message is subordinate to the technique.

47

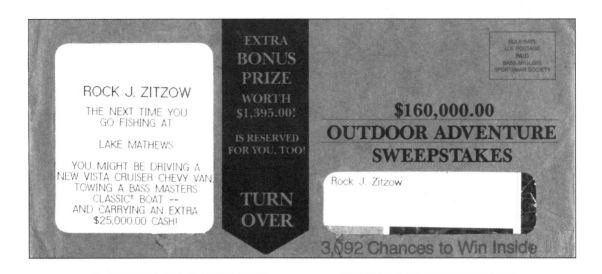

ROCK J. ZITZOW

THE NEXT TIME YOU
GO FISHING AT

LAKE MATHEWS

YOU MIGHT BE DRIVING A
NEW VISTA CRUISER CHEVY VAN,
TOWING A BASS MASTERS
CLASSIC® BOAT --
AND CARRYING AN EXTRA
$25,000.00 CASH!

But you don't have to catch the
Big One to be a big winner in
this sweepstakes, Rock J. Zitzow!

You're ALSO eligible to win one of
3,091 other great outdoor prizes,
too. Prizes like:

A Ranger Model 360V Comanche
boat with all the extras the Zitzow
family could ask for.

New Humminbird electronic
equipment that positively identifies
fish in red.

Three new rod and reel combos
that will make Rock J. Zitzow the
envy of his buddies. And still
more!

Just return all six Sweepstakes
Entry Certificates at the right and
maybe I'll call you some day soon
to say, "Rock J. Zitzow, YOU
JUST WON OUR GRAND PRIZE
WORTH $72,000.00!"

And why not take this chance to
accept a no-risk trial membership
in the Bass Anglers Sportsman
Society, too?

Rock J. Zitzow belongs in B.A.S.S.
And to prove it to you, we're
offering you 10 big membership
benefits ... a chance at a bonus
gift ... and a money-back offer!

You'll never have a better chance
to see why 536,000 of your
fellow bass fishermen avidly
support B.A.S.S., so why not try us
out?

See for yourself how B.A.S.S. can
help you enjoy the fishing at
LAKE MATHEWS, other hot spots
in CALIFORNIA and anywhere else
the lunkers bite!

Just check the "YES" box on the
bottom Certificate at right and our
members-only magazine,
BASSMASTER®, will soon begin
arriving at the Zitzow home 10
times each year.

Figures 4-3 and 4-4

A similar computer-personalized mailing, but because the mailer acknowledges the recipient goes fishing at Lake Mathews, this mailing uses technology to *connect* with the person who receives this mailing.

Why Bulk Doesn't Hack It in the 1990s

Thirty years ago it might have been possible to introduce a product by saturating the media with the brand name.

No more. It's inefficient, it's too expensive, and it ignores one vital component of the marketing mix: Competition. In the 1990s we have to tailor not only our products, but the advertising that sells our products, to each individual market group.

And that's what target marketing is.

Effective advertising isn't about brand names. It's about benefits. What will it do for *me*? Targeted marketing has to crash through or vault over a barrier of pre-existing opinions. So to put together a convincing sales argument, we have to know not only *who* our prospects are, we have to know what they want.

True "marketers" understand the most important strategic rule for winning the marketing war as we approach the twenty-first century. We have to match our message to our market group.

As consumers become more sophisticated, they expect advertisers to talk with them individually—one to one. Smart marketers know this. They modify their databases—and their advertising—so they can target a specific group of logical potential buyers.

HYPER-Targeting: Squeezing Out That Extra Drop of Response

If a marketer who died in 1960 was somehow resuscitated in 1990, he'd be surprised at the reply when he orders a Coca-Cola.

"You want Classic Coke? Diet Coke? New Coke? Cherry Coke? Diet Cherry Coke? Caffeine-free Coke? Or Diet Caffeine-Free Coke?"

The clerk has no idea how to pinpoint just who this guy is. If he did, he'd serve up a Classic Coke without confusing the buyer, because he'd know: Classic Coke is what this customer wants to drink because to *him* that's what Coca-Cola is.

If we project this reality into the world of marketing in print, mail, and broadcast—the 1990s world, with fragmented target-groups—we don't have to look beyond the immediate horizon to realize:

> *HYPER-targeting* has become the way to squeeze out that extra drop of response, the drop that more and more defines the difference between success and failure. Conventional media can't HYPER-target as specifically as direct marketing can, because only direct marketing is one-on-one.

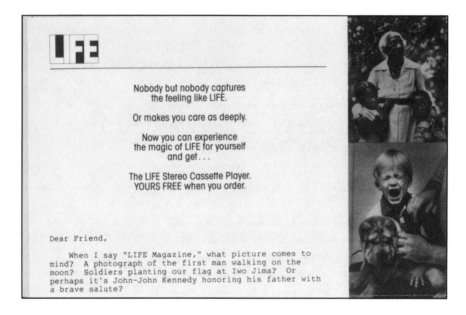

Figure 4-5

This mail package fairly screams out, "Premium!"

So <u>do</u> let us hear from you <u>today</u>.

With all best wishes,

Rachel Greenfield

Rachel Greenfield
Circulation Director

RG:ctrl

P.S.   <u>Don't forget</u> to peel off the "Free Stereo Cassette
       Player" token and affix it to your order card. It
       guarantees shipment of your FREE GIFT within 30-90
       days.

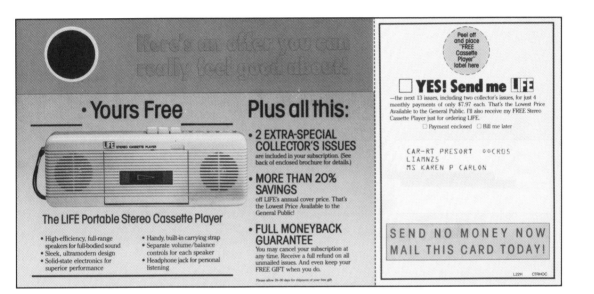

51

12 PICTURES THAT TELL YOU A LOT ABOUT

Bulk Rate
U.S. Postage
PAID
LIFE
Magazine

Plus your chance to receive 13 big issues—and a stereo tape deck, <u>free!</u>

(Available with your order—see details inside.)

LIAJGT2
KATE SALOVAARA

Figure 4-6

This mail package includes the premium, but its main emphasis is on the pictures in the magazine.

Detach here and mail in the postpaid envelope

LIFE
RSVP

SEND NO MONEY, unless you prefer. To get 13 big issues—plus this free stereo tape deck, just detach and mail this card in the postage-paid envelope.

FULL MONEY BACK GUARANTEE. You may cancel your subscription at any time and receive a full and prompt refund on all unmailed issues. You'll even keep your free gift!

L105F

☐ **YES! I'll try LIFE!** Send me the next 13 issues—including two extra-special collector's issues—for just four monthly payments of only $7.97 each. That's the lowest rate available to the general public, and I'll also receive my stereo tape deck—*free*—just for mailing my RSVP.

I may cancel my subscription at any time and receive a full refund on all unmailed issues. I'll even keep my free gift.

LIAJGT8
KATE SALOVAARA

MAIL THIS CARD TODAY! MDI

53

Which "LIFE" Do You Read?

I met a writer who was involved with subscription promotions for *LIFE* magazine years ago, when *LIFE* and *LOOK* were battling for supremacy in the picture-magazine field.

"We pitched noncompetitively, of course," he said. "Lester Suhler, the guru of subscription mailings was at *LOOK*, testing weird elements such as envelope colors. Who were the targets? A reader was a reader. *Everybody* was our target."

What uncomplicated golden days!

LIFE, now resurrected, fights for subscribers...against its sister magazines at Time, Inc., and against every other publication listed in category twenty-two of the consumer magazine issue of SRDS (Standard Rate & Data Service). *LIFE*—and every other general-interest magazine— also fights against television, a swarm of special-interest consumer magazines, and indifference in general.

I'm looking at three separate subscription packages for *LIFE*. Each is a "subscriber recruitment" mailing. Each differs from the others, slightly, in its aim. Each is a token move toward HYPER-targeting, which in my opinion is the absolute key to successful *reaching*, not just during this critical decade but coincidental with each inevitable and brutal postal and rate-card increase.

All three packages offer the same premium, a stereo cassette player— but the design and copy in the first package (figure 4-5) fairly scream out, "PREMIUM!" It bursts through the window on the envelope, it shouts in the overline of the letter, the P.S. exhorts us not to forget it, and the premium is the big-screen feature of the response device.

HYPER-targeting would call for this package to be aimed at subscribers known to respond to premium offers. I'd also test it against a non-premium version when mailed to others.

The second package (figure 4-6) includes the premium, but the main emphasis is *pictures*. The two brochures are full of pictures. Historical pictures. Fashion pictures. Pictures that chronicle. Pictures that tell a story. The copy talks about pictures. The brochure is pictures. The magazine bills itself as the "pictorial record of our times." The logical targets of figure 4-6 are: those who remember the "old" *LIFE*, and/or those who like "coffee-table" magazines.

The third package (figure 4-7) is a carnival of celebrities. If features Lady Di on the envelope and launches right into other celebrities. The package offers the same premium, but it also promises a "peek into the private notebooks Richard Burton left behind" and a visit with a "real-life Mafia Godfather." If we think of *targeting*, how much more tightly can we aim at movie-goers, TV-watchers, and *People*-readers?

Three separate package tests...in the early 1990s, it's still a reasonably sophisticated way to pick a winner. By the late 1990s these won't be tests; they'll be rollouts, results of pre-tests to *specific sub-groups*.

54

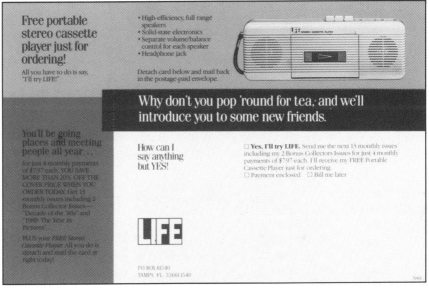

Figure 4-7

This mail package focuses on celebrities. It's logical to aim this sales message to People *magazine readers, movie-goers, and TV-watchers.*

Reaching Inside the Reader's Field of Interest

A HYPER-Targeting Warning: Make no selective assumptions beyond the known similarities within your target group.

Here's what I mean. There are two reasons for the mistakes now made in mis-aimed communications. The first is *flawed database interpretation*.

This version takes a database and misreads it based on preconceived personal prejudices or technical ignorance.

(What a joke the whole concept would be to the marketer of the 1970s who probably would not only have no notion of what we're talking about, but who, wallowing in the rich sea of data through which we swim, would see *no* need for assumptions beyond known demographic/psychographic profiles.)

The second reason for missing a target is *non-database interpretation*. This version ignores basic demographic/psychographic profiles entirely.

Figure 4-8 is the front of a subscription package envelope for a women's magazine which claims as its readership the "mature woman."

Two mechanical tricks catch our attention. We all know why the writer put them there: because they usually increase response, no matter what the offer is.

One is visible through the window. We see, "I accept." "I decline." Some psychologists say this increases response because it tells the reader: "You're in command."

The other is, "The favor of a reply is requested." This tends to increase response because it touches the reader's sense of guilt if she doesn't respond.

The key copy on this envelope:

> A special invitation to a woman who has reached the interesting age.

So far, so good. Everyone wants to be considered interesting. We turn the envelope over (figure 4-9) to read a quote from fashion doyenne, Coco Chanel:

> A woman does not become interesting until she is over 40.

Let's suppose this mailing reached a number of women under age forty. It did, by the way, which means either the list company made some mistakes *or* this publisher's research said women under forty are interested in having the sophistication of women over forty.

If it *wasn't* a mistake...then the message inside the envelope has to reinforce the reason for mailing to women under forty. To the HYPER-targeter this means using two separate lists, writing two separate copy slants, and tailoring the message and offer to each market group.

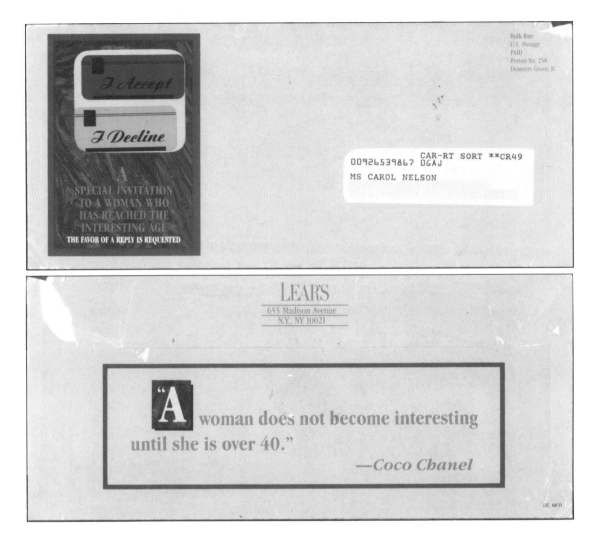

Figures 4-8 and 4-9

Since this package was mailed to a number of women under forty, the message on the inside of the envelope has to reinforce the reason for targeting that group of women. The copy should be tailored to the market group so that every reader's reaction is, "They mean me."

In this case, the magazine didn't pay any attention to the age differential. The message mailed to women under forty is identical to the message mailed to women over forty. In fact, in my opinion this opening is a killer to women under *fifty*:

> Congratulations! You've been a daughter, perhaps a student, a bride, a mother, a career women, a divorcee, a community leader, a widow, a grandmother.

How many recipients said, "Not *me*"?

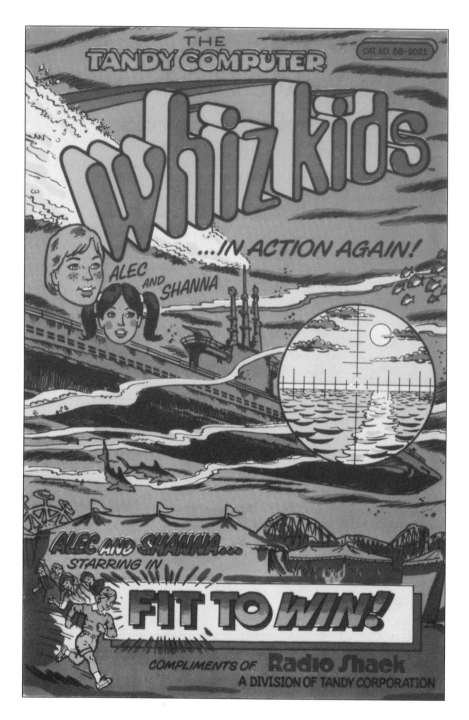

Figure 4-10

How to get an advertisement across to kids: Use a medium they're comfortable with. In this case, Radio Shack created a non-threatening comic book to show kids computers are easy to use.

Reaching "Impossible" Targets

A lot of target groups are almost impossible to reach. Kids, for instance. How do we get a message to them without losing their interest?

The easiest answer: We choose a medium specifically identifiable by their own age group.

Figure 4-10 shows how a computer company successfully gets kids interested in its product—a comic book. Not only does the advertiser place a formal ad in the comic book, but the entire action-adventure-mystery story within the book makes the product the hero. The story weaves itself around the kids featured in the story—and how they solved their mystery with the help of the computer. And within the disarming, non-threatening format of a comic book, computers appear easy to use. So instructional contents (computer tips and tricks) stick with the same comic book format.

Figure 4-11 is a mailing for a health care company. The quotes on the envelope read, "I think it's about time someone did something about ris-

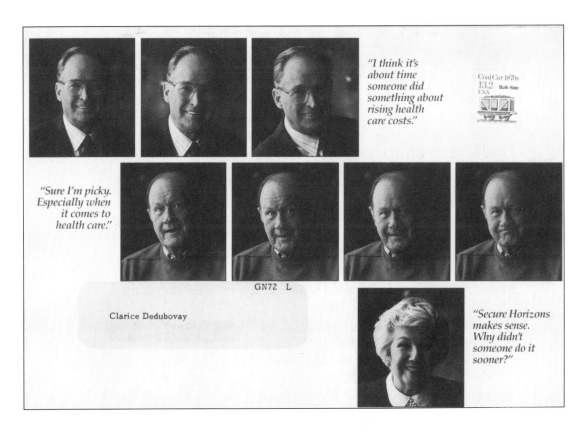

Figure 4-11

An appropriate piece of advertising targeted to senior citizens.

SecureHorizons
Health care for today's senior.

P.O. Box 26289
Santa Ana, CA 92799

Bulk Rate
US Postage
PAID
Permit #15
Santa Ana, CA

MISS CAROL NELSON

Figure 4-12

A not-so-appropriate piece of advertising mailed to someone who isn't a senior citizen. The copy is written to address a senior citizen—the message misses its target.

ing health care costs.'' ''Sure, I'm picky. Especially when it comes to health care.'' ''Secure Horizons makes sense. Why didn't someone do it sooner?''

The mailing addresses the health concerns of senior citizens and the photographs underscore the target group the company is addressing. This is a perfectly appropriate piece of HYPER-targeted advertising when they're addressing my grandmother—but not for someone in her mid-thirties. Take a look at Figure 4-12. The look of the package has changed, but even though the recipient isn't a senior citizen, the copy still addresses a senior citizen.

We have to assume this marketer suffers from either *flawed* or *non*-database interpretation. Which one? Who cares? When a bullet misses its target, it's a miss, regardless of whether the gun or the ammunition was faulty.

It's an easy fix, though. What do you do? You correct the sights on your list-selection rifle by targeting the mailing to someone younger than a senior citizen—the daughter or granddaughter of someone getting on in years. You polish your word-bullets by targeting the copy on the assumption your recipient is responsible for the health care costs of her mother or grandmother.

If we can increase response, even incrementally, by tailoring the sales message to the target...if we can get the reader to respond to our sales pitch by saying, ''They're talking to me''...that extra response will more

60

than pay for the extra time it took to create a well-thought-out, well-targeted sales message.

The point of all this: We *have to* analyze each communication on the logical 1990s basis. We should be keeping score the way any ongoing business keeps score: Does this message help sell a product or service to the intended customer, the targets who actually can use what we're selling?

A technical writer can write words about what we're selling. When we as salespeople tailor a message to specific readers, viewers, or listeners, we're writing not just copy but our own insurance policy against the reader glancing at our message and saying, "That's not me," just before tossing it into the round file, flipping the page, or switching the dial.

The Key to Targeting

To target during the mid-1990s we literally have to split the atom. We split each group again and again—in direct mail, vertical magazines, and even vertical television and radio stations. As each group becomes smaller and smaller, we still should be able to fine-tune the same offer within each subgroup.

A word of caution: In order to maximize impact within a selected group, we have to take great care not to *exclude* any members of that group. This means shaping the message like an exquisite sculpture. Every recipient must say, "They mean me."

Let's look at an early marriage of conventional media and direct marketing—some direct response space advertising.

Figure 4-13 is an ad for the L.L. Bean catalog. It ran in a general-interest news publication, *Newsweek*.

What specific target-group of logical potential buyers does this message reach? *Newsweek* readers have more money than the average person. That's a specific, if only because magazine subscribers have more money than the general population. But the magazine has a mass-audience appeal. Doctors read it, lawyers read it, housewives read it, students read it. That isn't so specific, *except* as a modifier to the recognition that *Newsweek* readers tend to have more money than the average person.

The headline, "The Golden Rule of L.L. Bean," isn't particularly dynamic. In fact, it's so un-dynamic the casual reader won't know what this advertiser wants him to do.

Figure 4-14 shows two connected response cards bound into the maga-

Figures 4-13 and 4-14

The headline on the ad, ''The Golden Rule of L.L. Bean,'' isn't particularly dynamic—but the response cards and coupon make it easy for the reader to respond.

zine, adjacent to the advertisement. Here is a development which certainly will come to full flower during the 1990s. You can see the ad has its own coupon. Why, then, have two additional means of response?

Why? Because in the 1990s the advertiser who wants a reader to respond does everything he can to make it easy for the reader to respond.

This ad appeared in a September issue, so the copy and the catalogs are geared to winter apparel. . . winter sports equipment. . . and accessories. . . for men and women who enjoy the outdoors.''

We have a general upscale message, aimed at the generalized upscale readership of *Newsweek*.

Figure 4-15 is another L.L. Bean ad. The company placed this one in a women's magazine. In a women's magazine we have ways to write an appeal to women we'd never in a million years use when we advertise to men *and* women.

Does L.L. Bean use *any* of those ways? In this ad, for some reason, no. In fact, the copy in this ad has no gender. Only the photographs underscore the placement of this generalized ad in a women's magazine.

But now look at the offer on the bind-in card adjacent to this ad (figure 4-16): ''Free *Women's* Catalog.'' The card is the response device, the moment of truth.

Figures 4-15 and 4-16

A token move toward targeting: The ad underscores its placement in a women's magazine through pictures only, but the response card shouts it loud and clear, "Free Women's Catalog."

> Too many marketers forget a concept that automatically increases or decreases response: The response device which adds reader-comfort by restating both the specific offer and the specific target will pull better than the response device which bypasses specifics.

The placement of this ad in a women's magazine, like the placement of the one in *Newsweek*, is *implicitly* targeted. But any women's magazine is automatically far more targeted, because the readership itself is more specific: We know more about the reader of this magazine than we know about the reader of the general news magazine. If she's active and outdoor-oriented, and reading this magazine, she's the logical target for this message.

Why isn't it logical to run the women's ad and cards in the general news publication we just saw? Obviously, because of the waste. At least half of *Newsweek* readers wouldn't be interested in this offer at all. And the half who would be interested—women—couldn't be as motivated to respond,

Figures 4-17 and 4-18

Selective binding now makes it possible for advertisers to personalize a message to a subscriber inside the magazine. Is this useful in a general-interest magazine? Or does the technique override the message?

because the ambience of *Newsweek* isn't as good a mirror for this message.

That's half the battle . . . Aiming at the right target. The other half: Using the right arrow.

The 1990s in Action

Figures 4-17 and 4-18 are two more examples of targeted bind-in cards in a magazine—only this time, instead of targeting a specific market group, they're HYPER-targeting a specific individual. The 1990s in action!

A growing number of magazines already offer ads personalized with the individual subscriber name. The name for this process is "Selective Binding." The magazine can now bind in these cards, and, using ink-jet printing, create ads "personalized" to the magazine's subscribers.

Even narrower targeting: personalizing on the ad itself.

We're going to see a lot of this during the 1990s because this technique can combine a personalized message with an ad targeted to a geographical region or demographic group.

In figures 4-17 and 4-18, Isuzu is selling a truck. This appeared in *Time*, a general-interest news magazine similar to *Newsweek*. So what do we know about the subscriber? We know this person has more money than average.

If our computer is sophisticated enough, we know the gender of the reader—perhaps. Michael and John are men, and Karen is a woman. Kim and Lee? Oh, well...

And we know the geographical area where this reader gets the magazine. You can see: This technique is as yet unperfected because we don't know whether this is her home or her office. If we had that information, we could tailor the message even more closely. (Subscription follow-ups already are enhancing the databases.)

In the 1990s, this whole concept is a miracle of targeting. But look ahead for a moment to the year 2001. By then a message to this woman will probably include *really* personal targeting with copy reflecting the answers to questions such as:

- How old is she? Junior year in college? Is she a senior citizen? Mother of a teen-ager?
- What does she do for a living? Is she a business-woman? Is she a clerk in a grocery store? Does she work in a factory?
- How does she spend her free time? Does she take the Girl Scout troop camping? Does she play tennis? Does she stay at home and knit?
- Family? Three children, three dogs, three canaries—or nothing?

Before we get too carried away with what the future holds, a question: Do we *want* to run a personalized ad in a general-interest news magazine?

The answer is—maybe.

The "maybe" depends on what we're selling.

The product they're selling here is a "...tough off-road vehicle with room to spare...it's big. With room for five adults."

The bind-in card (figure 4-18) offers a free gift. If our subscriber will test drive this truck, she gets her choice of a videotape (political thriller movie or sports documentary) or a designer telephone. In a general-interest magazine where we know the name of the subscriber but don't know *who* that person is, the advertiser has to offer more than one free-gift incentive.

Another 1990s development: Personalization on the card includes the participating dealer nearest our subscriber's address. It's amazing how far we've come from the words we had to use until just this decade—"See your nearest dealer."

How could an ad this targeted miss? Let's play devil's advocate for a moment.

Let's say we're acquainted with the woman who received this particular issue of *Time*.

She happens to be in the market for a car, so she's a potential customer. For the sake of argument:

She's seventy-six years old.

She knits.

She has no children.

She lives in the city.

Which total to...

She wouldn't be caught dead in any vehicle resembling a truck, especially, as the ad pitches at her, "a tough, off-road vehicle with room to spare."

She reads *Time* religiously, but why would she look twice at this ad?

Having her "notice" the ad doesn't help, because no one has made this ad relevant to her, and we haven't offered her enough options to make the sale.

> Getting attention isn't parallel to getting the sale. This *has to be* a growing recognition during this decade.

Certainly by the year 2001 an advertiser can anticipate no-problem personalization of the ad itself as well as the subscriber name. So we won't be selling trucks to seventy-six-year-old women. But what can we do today, struggling through the crucial 1990s?

How to Appeal to the Biggest Possible Target-Group

If we're looking for a wide audience, and we place our ad in a general-interest publication, we do have ways to be certain we appeal to the biggest possible target-group.

When readership is nonspecific, enlarge the target. Advertise the product which appeals to the broadest cross section of readership.

If that technique doesn't appeal to you, and you want to target part of the readership, cover the other readers with a secondary offer.

Using these yardsticks, how could we have saved this ad without changing the product? Simple: Build in options so the ad appeals to a wider audience.

First, if our reader isn't interested in this particular model, make sure she knows she can still get her free gift if she test drives a different model car. Showing different models at the bottom of the ad would have been easy.

Second, if she's not in the market for a car right now but knows someone who is, tell her she can pass this coupon to her interested friend, even though the ad is personalized in her own name.

Don't let novel technology take over where you should have a strong, well-thought-out selling message. Communications-strength lies in combining technology with a strong, well-thought-out sales message.

If we personalize randomly, we run two risks. The first is the risk of destroying any trace of rapport we might otherwise have established with the reader.

The second risk is even greater: The cost-per-thousand is more than double that of a conventional, nonpersonalized full-page ad. If we're going to pay this kind of premium for our personalized ad, we'd better be absolutely certain we're increasing response beyond the extra cost.

Using selective binding can be like adding jet fuel to our advertising, but only if we use it properly.

An Even More Exact Way for the Creative Team to Target a Market

Working Woman is a magazine targeted to female business executives. If we want to market an automobile to this particular group of women, what kind of car would it be, and how would we write our sales appeal?

In figure 4-19 Chevrolet matches not only product but sales appeal to the reader of this magazine.

The ad shows a racy red convertible and a striking-looking professional woman (shown far more prominently than the car...why?). The headline: Because the one who gets there first wins.

Check the targeting of this copy. It talks about not getting left behind and the importance of having power when you need it.

This message is aimed like an arrow, not only at the business woman, but at any woman who wants a car with power under the hood. And that's the trigger word: "power"...because it bleeds over into the individual's estimation of herself. Copy matches the readership of this magazine.

Would a personalized bind-in card accompanying this ad have generated better-qualified leads than the last ad we looked at? Probably, because the writers of this ad know whom they're talking to. They reach the reader by making the advertising *relevant* to the reader.

Chevrolet integrated this ad into a total campaign. Figure 4-20 is the envelope.

Figure 4-21 is front and back of the brochure of a mailing to a list of professional women. To us armchair critics, signature copy for both ad and mailer could be stronger. "The Heartbeat of America...Today's Chevrolet." Haven't we, as typical targets, asked for years: What does it mean?

(Would the writer of this ad buy a car from a Chevrolet dealer if, after asking the dealer, "What's so special about this car, and what makes it better than Ford or Toyota?" the limp answer came staggering back: "It's the heartbeat of America"?)

Ignoring this mild aberration, the integration of ad and mailer has a synergistic effect.

> Doubling the exposure by sending mail to the same people who see your media advertisement increases the pull of *both*.

For clarity of point, a direct comparison. *McCall's* is another women's magazine. But its audience is a different group of women: those with families and children.

Figure 4-22 is another Chevrolet ad, but this one was placed in *McCall's*. See the difference in targeting?

The ad this advertiser placed in *Working Woman* wouldn't work as well in *McCall's*. Why not? Because the woman reading *McCall's*—and don't forget she might be the same woman who reads *Working Woman*—has a different mind-set while reading this magazine. She's *far* more likely to be thinking traditionally: She's planning tonight's dinner or deciding on new school shoes for little Johnny or making arrangements for Bonnie's fifth birthday party.

Why do we assume this? Because otherwise, she'd still be reading *Working Woman*; she wouldn't be reading *McCall's*.

We "advertising professionals" are supposed to lead the way in targeting. And we've begun to realize we can sell almost anything if the message and the medium match the reader.

That's the "upgrade" from the 1980s: Message, medium, and market —all three have to match.

One last example of targeting.

In the 1980s, if we knew we were writing to a single coherent group of

Chevrolet, Chevy and the Chevrolet emblem are registered trademarks of GM Corp. © 1988 GM Corp. All Rights Reserved.   Let's get it together...buckle up. GM

Figure 4-19

This ad targets not only the product but the sales appeal to the reader of a women's business magazine. Would a personalized bind-in card reach the intended audience better than in a general-interest magazine?

Because the one who gets there first, wins.

Fairy tales of the tortoise and the hare aside, slow and steady doesn't get you anywhere but left behind. But no one can go all out, all the time either. The answer: Conserve your energy until you need it, then put on a burst of speed. All it takes is a measure of power.

With cars, there are two measures of engine power potential: horsepower and torque. Essentially, horsepower measures speed potential and torque measures acceleration potential. When evaluating

a car's performance, look at *both* figures. If they're roughly equal, the car may feel sluggish, as the engine labors to bring you up to speed. But when torque is the higher of the two, your car's response is eager, powerful. Gratifying.

In a Cavalier Z24 convertible, you'll get the all-systems-are-go combination of 130 horsepower and 165 ft.-lbs. of torque. All at a great Chevy price. So you'll have a powerful advantage. And the others will have a lot of catching up to do.

THE *Heartbeat* OF AMERICA — TODAY'S CHEVROLET™

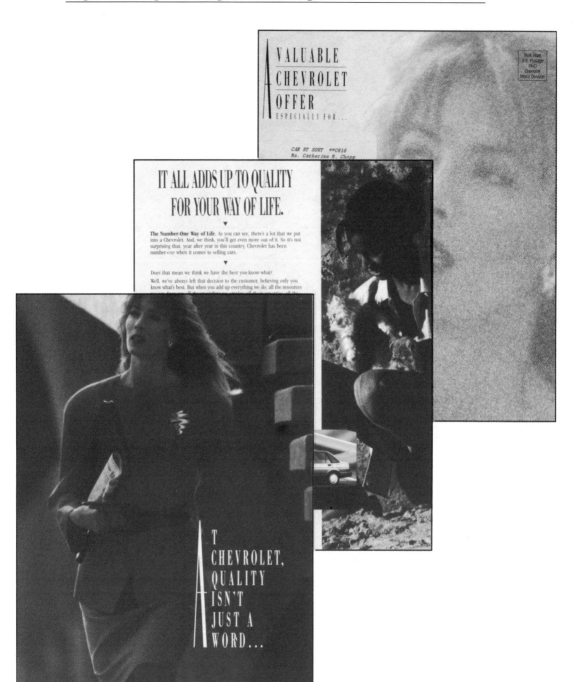

Figures 4-20 and 4-21

Chevrolet integrated their message into a total campaign by mailing this package to a list of professional businesswomen. The integration of ad and mailer has a synergistic effect when it doubles the exposure of the advertising message.

people (in this case, alumni of a college) we'd have thought we had plenty of ammunition to target our message.

But these are the 1990s.

Take a look at figures 4-23 and 4-24. They appear to be parallel shots at the same targets—Boston College alumni.

Figure 4-23 is an envelope telling the recipient, "Enclosed: *New* opportunities for select Boston College alumni only." The other envelope, figure 4-24, says, "An *exclusive* opportunity for Boston College alumni only."

Before we open the envelopes, let's ask ourselves, What's the purpose of sending two different mailings to the same group?

The answer: They *aren't* the same group. The envelope with the legend "Enclosed: New opportunities" is aimed at individuals who still are involved in college activities. These people attend sports events and concerts. They still identify themselves with the school.

The envelope with the legend "An exclusive opportunity" is aimed at individuals who attended the school, graduated, and then forgot about it. The college has their current mailing address, but these alumni aren't "active."

Inside the envelopes (figures 4-25 and 4-26) we see identical offers. They both offer the same credit card. The letter to active alumni is based on pride—the pride of being an alumnus of this college. In fact, the word "pride" is a key word in the copy.

The letter to inactive alumni is more reserved. Instead of pride, the thrust is exclusivity. In fact, the word "exclusive" is a key word in the copy.

The brochures (figures 4-27 and 4-28) carry through the same theme. To active alumni, we write about tradition: "Carry this and you carry on the Boston College tradition." To inactive alumni, we stay on a safe course—exclusivity: "A credit line as high as $25,000 because you're a privileged member of the Boston College community."

Take a Hard Look

A suggestion: If you have any responsibility for writing or placing your advertising, take a hard look at the publications you're going into and the lists you're using. Who is going to read what you write? Who is going to identify with or reject your illustrations?

And take that look *before* you write your message.

We have to match our message to our market because doing this increases our chances for a sale. And increasing our chances for a sale is why people hire us in the first place.

Does this mean the end of direct mail letters using the standard greeting, "Dear Friend"?

I hope so. Believe me it won't be missed.

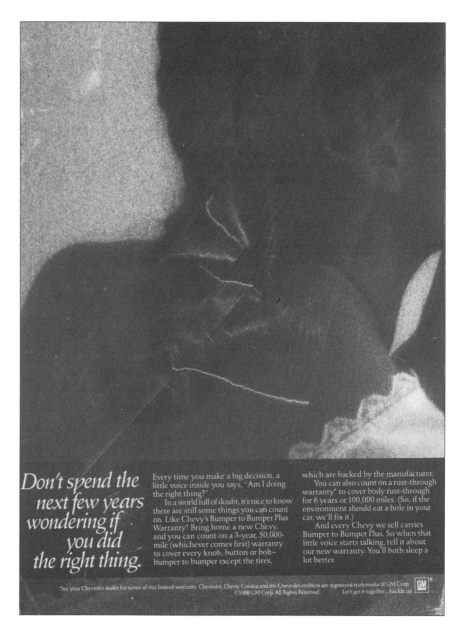

Figure 4-22

Another ad placed in a magazine whose audience is women with families and children. Compare the targeting with figure 4-19.

Figures 4-23 and 4-24

Both these envelopes appear to be targeting the same audience. But *are* they?

BOSTON COLLEGE ALUMNI ASSOCIATION
825 CENTRE STREET NEWTON, MA 02158

Dear Sample,

As a select Alumni member of Boston College, you're eligible for the Boston College Alumni Association Privileged Banking Visa® card.

This card is offered only to the Boston College alumni community, through a unique arrangement with Shawmut Bank, N.A. It's a perfect way to show your pride in your college and continue to help your alumni association.

The Boston College Alumni Association Privileged Banking Visa card gives you a high line of flexible credit. It also gives you a good way to support your college: Every time you use your Privileged Banking Visa to make a purchase, Shawmut Bank pays a percentage to your alumni association. Plus, a portion of each annual membership fee is donated each year to the Boston College Alumni Association.

As a Boston College graduate, you're entitled to a credit card with special extra advantages -- advantages you won't find with ordinary cards:

- A low variable annual percentage rate (currently just 16.86%).

- Free additional cards for your family members.

- 24-hour cash access to your credit line.

- Personalized loan checks at no additional cost.

As a distinguished member of the Boston College community, your annual fee is waived for the first six months. The enclosed brochure describes your benefits in more detail.

BC

Dear Sample,

You're part of the select circle of individuals eligible to apply for an exceptional card: The Boston College Alumni Association Privileged Banking Visa® card.

Carry this card -- proudly featuring the Boston College Eagle -- and you show your exclusive alliance with this respected group of alumni.

As a member of this special circle, you're entitled to special extra advantages -- advantages you won't find with ordinary cards. Through our unique arrangement with Shawmut Bank, N.A., you can now carry the card that gives you:

- A low variable annual percentage rate (currently just 16.86%).

- Free additional cards for your family members.

- 24-hour cash access to your credit line.

- Personalized loan checks at no additional cost.

And your annual fee is waived for the first 6 months.

On behalf of the Alumni Association, I invite you to carry this exceptional card. Take a moment to look over the enclosed brochure. It describes your benefits in more detail. Simply complete the short application and return it before September 29, 1989.

We'll be delighted to count you in as a member of the Boston College Alumni Association Privileged Banking Card circle.

Figures 4-25 and 4-26

Figure 4-25 is a letter to alumni who still proudly identify with the school. "Pride" is a key word in the copy. Figure 4-26 is a letter to a different group of alumni: They attended the school, but aren't "active." This letter is more reserved. Instead of "pride," "exclusive" is a key word in the copy.

79

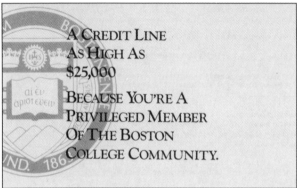

Figures 4-27 and 4-28

The brochures in each package carry through the same theme: One emphasizes tradition; the other emphasizes the privileged status of the alumnus.

Marketing Checklist — Chapter 4

☐ 1. Are you *connecting* with people in your advertising?

☐ 2. Is your sales message genuinely motivating to your market group? Or have you fallen in love with a technique?

☐ 3. Have you romanced the benefits of what you're selling?

☐ 4. Have you studied the database or available research about your target audience? Or have you ignored facts in favor of your own personal predjudice?

☐ 5. If you have separate and distinct large target groups for your message, have you modified your message to appeal to each group's specific interests?

☐ 6. Have you taken care not to hone your message down to the point where you exclude some of the people you want to reach?

☐ 7. If you want your reader to respond to your ad have you made it easy to respond?

☐ 8. Are your sales arguments specific? Is your response device specific?

☐ 9. Are you avoiding the mistake that ''getting attention'' is parallel to ''getting the sale?''

☐ 10. Are you aware of—but not in awe of—beneficial novel technology which helps you motivate your targets? Or have you let novel technology substitute for a strong, well-thought-out sales argument?

☐ 11. Have you integrated the media in your campaign, to increase the exposure of your advertising message?

CHAPTER 5

Harnessing Image and Direct into a Well-Matched Team

As direct marketing and conventional advertising marry each other—two warring ruling families achieving peace through joy—each must be aware of the weaknesses of the other, the reason for needing a marriage partner in the first place. The power resulting from a team-effort is impressive compared to the negative results of one partner going it alone.

Let's explore a weakness of conventional advertising: inability to convert a conventional ad to a direct response ad without losing coherence. And we'll tie it to one of direct marketing's weaknesses: hard-sell demand for an order with little or no regard for romance.

Lip Service, Confusion, and Eventual Happiness

Conventional print advertising has entered a new era...an era in which no general ad agency worth its standing in the "Red Book" feels it should expose itself to a client without adding direct response prominently to their list of services. Great start, but the union seems to be producing some pretty confusing advertising.

What makes it confusing is the practice of trying to turn any ad into a direct response sales generator. Stick a coupon onto a corner of an existing ad or throw in an 800 number and this is called a "direct response" ad.

Too often I've seen one creative group (the "conventional" group) create a full-page ad, and a different creative group (the "direct" group) create the coupon. They call this a marriage. Isn't it normal for the marital partners to at least be *introduced* to each other?

The Coupon Dilemma

Figure 5-1 is a full-page, 4-color ad in a women's magazine. Its headline: "No Deposits. No Returns." Ambiguous enough. Now, what are they selling?

The copy says: "If there's no stuck-on food or powder residue, there's no re-washing."

So what else is new? I already know that. That's why I have to scrape and double rinse all my dishes before they go into the dishwasher.

"Once is all it takes." The final line.

Okay. They're trying to sell automatic dishwasher soap. I figure this out from squinting really hard at the wording on the picture of the bottle, which, of course, has to be the product.

But wait—if I look at the coupon, I can win some cookware! VISIONS cookware—what's that? Is it what's pictured in the ad? No, no, that's dinnerware. So what *is* this cookware? And what does it have to do with this product? Who cares? Obviously not whoever wrote and laid out the text of the ad.

If I send in the coupon, I might win some cookware. But why does Palmolive want my name? Why would they give me cookware, for doing nothing?

Let's translate that question into marketing/database terms. Once the Palmolive people receive my coupon, what will they do with it? The only possible answer: Some researcher somewhere will put my name and address on a mailing list.

Yet, if *that's* the reason for this very expensive, very vague ad—list

Figure 5-1

Without the coupon, this ad is a non-message. The coupon adds a message, but doesn't relate to the ad.

information—how valuable will that information be to anyone? It doesn't say I use the product (since I haven't redeemed the coupon to buy it). It doesn't even say I have an automatic dishwasher. All it says about me is this: I have a name and an address and I was reading this magazine one day.

What happened here? Someone stuck a coupon onto an ad, inserted information *not* in the ad itself, and said, ''Now we have a direct response message.'' Without the coupon, the ad transmits no message at all; with the coupon, we have a message, but it leads nowhere because the coupon seems to have been pasted onto an ad—any ad.

Figure 5-2

Which computer does this advertiser single out? And which computer does the coupon offer information on? The reader is lost in a sea of unrelated messages.

> A response device should either a) recapitulate or emphasize the key message in the ad relative to why the coupon is there in the first place, or b) provide the advertiser with useful information about the respondent, or c) both.

The simplest test of coupon effectiveness is to disconnect the coupon, show the ad alone to an outsider, and ask what the coupon should include.

In figure 5-2, Tandy does a better job of showing me the product in a computer ad. Or do they? I can see this is a broad line of computers ("The broadest line of PCs in America"), but I believe they're trying to sell me just one here, the 1000 TL. Every word of copy describes this computer. OK, maybe I'll return the coupon to get more information.

Uh-oh. The coupon tells me they'll send me the "RSC-20 Computer Catalog." I want information on the Tandy 1000. At least I think I do, but by the time I decipher the coupon and, if I'm especially bright that day, interpret the "RS" of "RSC" as meaning "Radio Shack" (Is it? I'm still not sure, but I *am* sure I hate unexplained initials), I've given up and turned the page to the next ad.

A Clever Idea? Who Knows?

What if you walked into your office one morning and saw a huge piece of graffiti covering your filing cases? Your secretary sits traumatized, obviously having gone off the deep end. Papers are everywhere.

Probably you'd mutter, "Excuse me," leave, and come back tomorrow, when the nightmare might be over.

I've described the illustration in figure 5-3, which takes up about 60 percent of a full-color ad. The headline:

> Nobody likes it, but some of us have learned to hate it
> less.

The "it" apparently is *filing*. So what's the message?

For a reason not explained in the text, this company has established an "I Hate Filing" club. (Put that membership in your resume, folks!) We see three items above the coupon. They're a booklet called "How to File"; a teddy bear; and a cup with "I Hate Filing" emblazoned in red.

It's the coupon that puzzles me. The copy reads:

> Just fill in and mail this coupon to "I Hate Filing" Club, 71
> Clinton Road, Garden City, NY 11530. Please print
> clearly.

Figure 5-3

*What's the message here? The reader is engaged by a free membership,
but discouraged by a coupon that doesn't spell out membership benefits.*

All right, what's the relationship between this booklet, the teddy bear
and the cup? I'm intrigued by a membership that seems to cost nothing,
but disenchanted by a coupon that doesn't seem to relate to any specifics.

Another approach to merging general advertising and direct response
in print advertising is through the use of bind-in card inserts. As I said in
the previous chapter, we're going to be seeing more and more hard-
working response inserts in the 1990s because they're an excellent way to
combine attractive, eye-catching graphics with a potent sales message

The inserts are often as well-designed as the ad itself—and if they're
done right you know at one glance they're *part* of the ad.

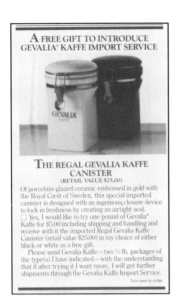

Figure 5-4

The four-color card insert gives the reader an incentive to order, but what if someone removed the card? The casual reader may not read past the undynamic headline of the ad—even if he does, the body copy never mentions the $5 offer.

Don't Forget the "Pass-Along" Value of Advertising

Figure 5-4 is an ad and bound-in insert for a fancy coffee. The ad's headline reads:

> Of the finer things Sweden makes, the finest may be its coffee.

Pretty *un*dynamic puffery.

What *is* dynamic about this ad is the insert bound in under the headline. It reads:

> A free gift to introduce Gevalia Kaffe Import Service.

The copy offers a ceramic coffee canister plus one pound of this fancy coffee for a $5.00 shipping and handling charge.

OK, now *that's* a good way to get a reader to try mail-order coffee. If the body copy in the ad sells the reader, he'll rip out the insert and mail it.

A well-integrated ad plus a bind-in card should at least double the anticipated response. If it doesn't the advertiser should examine both components for 1) congruence, 2) clarity, and 3) reader-instruction.

Have you ever come across a magazine ad which refers to a bind-in card ...and all you see is the stump where the card used to be? If that were the case with this fancy coffee ad, you probably wouldn't have glanced at this ad *at all*.

Why? Because when the first reader ripped out the insert, he ripped out the guts of this ad. All that is left is the *un*dynamic part of the ad.

The first line of body copy reads, "The words 'made in Sweden' have always stood for uncompromising quality and artistry." C'mon, we're talking about *coffee* here! A major benefit is buried deep in the text: "Roasted faster, it's then vacuum-sealed faster...because even the finest whole beans rapidly grow stale when exposed to air, as in gourmet shop bins." Now *that's* a reason to buy *this* coffee. Let's hope the reader gets that far.

If the full-page ad had a headline that pulled the reader down into the copy...and if the copy hadn't been artificially puffed up for almost half a page, the next reader might continue to read and see the *benefits* of ordering this coffee by mail, even without the missing card.

90

But that second reader probably missed the second offer of a free canister because it's cleverly hidden from view in the body copy of the ad, and now the card isn't there to rescue.

Since the *only* way you can get this coffee is through the mail, this full page ad plus insert wasn't used to its full potential. Instead of assuming every reader is a potential customer, it deliberately set out to pull only one.

Now, of course, that isn't a *total* loss. In fact, if the card stimulated a trial order from a reader who wouldn't have responded had the card not been there, it's no loss at all. But as copywriters—as *marketers* our job is to maximize the use of expensive media that have pass-along potential, to bring in more than one customer from a single well-placed, well-thought-out ad.

Primary Readership Isn't the Only Readership

Another magazine falls open toward the back cover where we find the back-end of an insert for an airline (figure 5-5, bottom right).

You may have noticed that the bound-in backs of card inserts are sometimes just white paper. Not this one. The bold red copy reads:

> See the other end of this insert for details about a valuable travel offer from TWA.

How often have you seen a reader search through a magazine looking for an ad? Not too often, I'll wager. But this one, not surprisingly, does send the reader scurrying to find the other half of the insert.

The rest of figure 5-5 is what the reader finds: a card-insert bound adjacent to another TWA full-page ad.

The offer? A 25 percent discount coupon on TWA.

The next person who gets the magazine finds only the full-page ad—no insert—for TWA. The headline reads:

> 150 cities
> in 18 countries
> on 4 continents
> have one thing in common:
> Us.

Ok. It's a "me"-driven headline. And the body copy doesn't mention a 25 percent discount offer anywhere; it just tells the reader to call a travel agent or TWA at the toll-free number.

Another missed opportunity? Probably.

Figure 5-5

The other half of a bound-in insert (bottom right) sends the reader flipping through the magazine to find the travel offer. The bound-in insert was well-thought-out to the last detail, but the full-page ad is little more than image and doesn't even mention the offer.

TWA /ATLANTIC MONTHLY
25% DISCOUNT CERTIFICATE OFFER

ACT NOW to receive a 25% discount certificate from TWA® and Atlantic Monthly. The TWA® 25% Discount Certificate can be used to obtain a 25% discount on the purchase of a TWA and/or Trans World Express® (TWE) ticket for one-way or round-trip travel (coach fares booked in K and V class are excluded). Trans World Express flights operate with TWA flight numbers 7000-7999. Certificate is valid for any TWA destination in the United States and the Caribbean and from the United States to any TWA international destination excluding Cairo and Tel Aviv. Travel with the certificate is valid during the period September 1, 1990 through August 31, 1991. Certain holiday blackouts apply.

It's easy to receive your TWA/Atlantic Monthly 25% Discount Certificate. Just follow these simple steps:
1. Fill out legibly all the requested information on the order form. (Limit two certificates per household address). There is a postage and handling fee of $5.00, for a maximum of two certificates per household address.
2. Mail application along with check or money order for $5.00 made payable to:

TWA/Atlantic Monthly Travel Offer
P.O. Box 4000, Dept. AM
Plymouth Meeting, PA 19462

Your certificate(s) will be mailed to you. Requests must be postmarked by 6/30/90. Maximum two certificates per household address. Allow 3 to 4 weeks for delivery.

It's also easy to make your reservation and purchase tickets —just follow these simple steps:
1. After you receive your certificate(s), make your reservation at any TWA ticketing facility, travel agency or by calling TWA reservations at 1-800-221-2000 and advising the agent you hold a TWA/Atlantic Monthly 25% Discount Certificate. You must provide your certificate number when you call to make a reservation.
2. Purchase tickets at any authorized travel agency, TWA ticketing facility, or through TWA's Telemail (tickets-by-mail) service.

TWA/ATLANTIC MONTHLY 25% DISCOUNT CERTIFICATE ORDER FORM
1. Certificate(s) must be redeemed, and all travel must be completed by

midnight, August 31, 1991.
2. This offer may be used only with qualifying published adult fares filed by TWA.
3. Travel with the certificate is valid for tickets issued on TWA stock for travel on TWA and/or TWE only. Travel is not permitted on TWA-designated flights operated by other airlines.
4. Tickets issued against the certificate may not be combined with any other coupon, Frequent Flight Bonus Award ticket, other promotional offer, unpublished fare or upgrade program; it is not valid for use with travel industry employee discounts or with special travel programs, such as the Takeoff Pass® or Breakaway Club(sm).
5. Certificates are not transferable, not redeemable for cash, and cannot be applied to a credit card balance or used toward the purchase of a Miscellaneous Charge Order (MCO) or Prepaid Ticket (PTA).
6. Only one certificate may be used per ticket issued.
7. Certificate must be presented wh ¬ tickets are purchased. Certificate may be used to purchase tickets on   ¬ndividual named on the face of the certificate. Identificatic   ¬d at check-in. TWA has the final authority regarding
8. The following blackout dates   ¬¬ion
to those associated with the far
DOMESTIC:
1990: Nov. 21-26; Dec. 20-?
1991: Jan. 1-2
9. This certificate is not con¬ fares booked in K and V cl
10. Certificate use is subj¬ foreign governments an¬ Complete terms and c¬ certificate.

PLEASE TYPE OR PRINT LEGIBLY. COMPLETE ALL INFORM

Exact Name(s) to be Printed on Certificates:

1. _____

2. _____

PLEASE ENCLOSE:
1. Completed order form.
2. Check or money order made payable to: **TWA/Atlantic Monthly Travel Offer** for a $5.00 postage and handling fee for a maximum of 2 certificates per household address.

Name of Purchase

Address: _____

State: _____

MAIL TO:
TWA/Atla
P.O. Box 4¬
Plymouth¬
Allow 3 t¬

SEE THE OTHER END OF THIS INSERT FOR DETAILS ABOUT A VALUABLE TRAVEL OFFER FROM TWA

The way this reads, TWA seems to have thought it would have received the same number of responses, the same number of booked discounted seats, if the airline had run the insert only. If primary readership is the *only* desirable readership, why do magazines blow so many of their own subscription cards into the same issue?

Spiegel has a long history of combining inserts with attention-grabbing full-page ads. Figure 5-6 is an eye-catching ad. It shows a baby in the buff—except for an oversized bowler hat. The headline:

> The Breton Bowler.
> Now Available in Nurseries.

Now *that's* a mystery that pulls you down into the copy—copy which *almost* clears it up:

> Thanks to Spiegel, anywhere you can read, you can shop.

Mystery finally solved with the offer (in teeny-tiny print):

> For your copy of the Spiegel Fall Catalog, call toll-free...

Here's the kicker: An adjacent bound-in insert for ordering the catalog by mail.

But wait—the order insert says Spiegel will send a catalog *and* a $6 merchandise certificate *and* a free Crocodile Print Carryall *and* fast UPS delivery *and* free pickup on any returns.

But the sparse copy on the ad doesn't mention those extra benefits. The person who gets this magazine after the insert has been ripped out can't know about them. And they might be the extra benefits that clinch the pass-along sale. It's not as though there is enough room for the copy in the full-page ad. Why is the direct response insert expected to carry the full weight of response-salesmanship?

When You Want the Reader to Respond, Make It Easy for the Reader to Respond

Sometimes we run across an ad that, even though it cries out for a coupon or a bound-in card insert, has no means for the reader to respond at all.

Figure 5-7 is a public service ad. Note the headline:

"The problem isn't how little we care. The problem is how little we do about it."

Oh. How little we care about what? How little we do about what?

The second largest block of print says, "What you give is five. What

Figure 5-6

Spiegel's ads are well-written and eye-catching. But information on the insert, which isn't included in the ad, could mean they've lost a lead on a new customer.

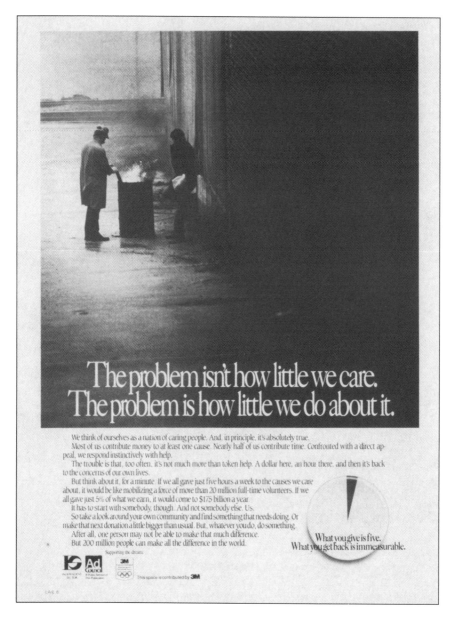

Figure 5-7

The problem isn't how little we care—the problem is we have no way to respond to this ad. If you want the reader to respond, make it easy *for the reader to respond.*

you get back is immeasurable.'' Well, gee, I've always wanted to get back something immeasurable—what five do they want? Five minutes? Five dollars? Five people to help? Five o'clock?

For the reader who is doggedly determined to find out what this ad is all about, tiny type tells us we do too little about our nation's problems and admonishes us for giving nothing more than token help.

Help for what? We're asked, mildly, to give time, money, caring, sharing of a human spirit...for what cause? This ad tells me I should be doing something but I don't have the foggiest idea where to start.

Wait a minute—there it is in lilliputian print buried in the middle of the gray copy block. Now I know what that five is I'm supposed to give. They want five hours or 5 percent of my income. Well, that makes it clear. But too late.

And, finally, they tell me that one person may not be able to make much of a difference, but 200 million people might. Does this mean *I* need to go out and find 200 million people to help me? Maybe, but I'll never know because this ad has no coupon or any means of responding. It's a full-page statement of muddy philosophy. Rather than trying to figure out how I'm supposed to respond, I've turned the page. So for all the money, time and good intentions spent on this ad, how can this message affect the reader's attitude...much less stir him into action?

This ad is typical of too many we're seeing while we wait for the marriage between conventional advertising and direct marketing to be consummated. It needs a response device because without some way of keeping score the communication is lost in limbo. It needs some kind—any kind—of call to action so it doesn't end up like so many ads, a mere waste of another tree branch in a sea of meaningless paper.

A Working Example of an Integrated Marketing Plan

For an illustration of how to harness both image and direct into a well-matched team, let's take a look at how a company might put together a typical integrated marketing plan. Let's say our product is called ''Fountain,'' a bottled water for home delivery. Our product can be ordered toll-free and delivered as often as our customers like. Our primary marketing objective: To increase home deliveries of our product.

To attain that objective, we decide on the image we'd like to project (example: Our water is clean, pure, and delivered fresh right to your doorstep).

We create ''traditional'' media (television, radio, magazine, newspaper) ads to project that image and, because our product can easily be ordered over the phone, it's natural to include a call to action—telling the reader/viewer/listener to pick up the phone and order our product.

How to Combine Image with Response

Let's assume our image creative is in place—enhanced by a call to action and a toll-free order phone number. We've made our television buy —our telephone operators are ready. Now what steps do we take to enhance sales?

If you immediately thought of "targeting,"—bingo! What types of people would be interested in our product and how would we reach them one-to-one? (Before reading on, why not make up your own list of logical targets and how *you* would reach them? Then you can check your suggestions against the actual presentation.)

Here's a sampling of possible choices we could make:

Dieters

Mail   — Use health club member lists, weight-watcher and diet-club lists, and diet book buyer lists.

Promotion — Install fountain water coolers in health clubs and dance studios at a discount to the club. Supply order forms or coupons on the sides of the coolers. Display 1-800 phone number prominently on coolers.
              — Joint promotion with powdered drink manufacturers.

Offer   — Videotape (made in-house) of:
                  Exercise routines (emphasizing the importance of water in a diet),
                  Low calorie cooking (with importance of water) including recipes and cooking demonstrations.

New Movers

Mail   — National Change of Address (NCOA) lists.

Offer   — Free one-month trial.

Health-Concerned Groups

Mail   — Environmental groups.
              — Vitamin mail-order buyers.

Promotion — (Seasonal): sponsor jogging, bike, and regional sports marathons (which entitles you to endorsement of the

98

activity—and, of course, you provide Fountain water at check points).

— Promote your health image by placing coolers in:

Doctors' offices with order cards and toll-free phone number.

Health food and upscale grocery stores with order cards and toll-free phone number.

Pharmacies with order cards and toll-free phone number.

New Business/Business-to-Business

Don't forget all those offices needing water coolers. Target your mail or sales effort to the purchasing manager or office manager.

Cooks

Mail   — *Food & Wine* subscribers (also regional Direct response ad buys with bound-in response form).
             — *Bon Appetit* subscribers (also regional Direct response ad buys with bound-in response form).

New Mothers

Mail   — ''Marriage mail'' insert into mailing targeted to new mothers.
             — List use plus buys in magazines such as *Parents* and *Working Mother*, with response card.

Parents/Families

Mail   — Parents magazine lists (also regional Direct response ad buys with bound-in response form).

Promotion — Joint promotion with Kool-Aid (doorknob hanger with offer of month's supply of Kool-Aid with sign up).
             — Co-op in-store offer of free Kool-Aid (Fountain offer in Kool-Aid packages).

These are just a few targets you could pinpoint. What other media come to mind when we pursue our marketing plan?

1. Selective binding—place a personalized response form in magazines.

99

2. Newspaper Free-Standing-Inserts (in the shape of the water bottles —so they stand out in the clutter of all those other FSIs) with toll-free 800 number.

3. Direct response outdoor boards—add the toll-free 800 number to reinforce radio direct response.

4. Direct response bus signboards.

5. Direct response bus placards with ''take-ones.''

Let's not forget a built-in sales vehicle: Since we have drivers delivering water, why not use them to distribute advertising? How would they do it? They can deliver:

1. A ''door-hanger'' ad to houses in the route which don't currently receive the product. This could consist of an ad and promotion for first-time buyers.

2. A ''bottle hanger'' ad placed on the bottle necks of deliveries to current customers: ''Tell a friend, get a gift'' promotion with incentive.

Let's not forget: Our product is a ''long-term'' product, that is, it's not like buying a shirt, wearing it out, and buying another one. It's continual service, continual delivery—so we want to not only get the customer to order, we want to make sure the customer continues to be happy with our product. We want to build an ongoing relationship with our customer. How do we do that?

By concentrating on more than the sale—concentrating on customer retention once we've made the initial sale. We have several ways to continue a dialogue with our customers. We can:

1. Create a Fountain customer magazine/newsletter (include line extensions, monthly promos, water information, recipes, environmental concerns).

2. Remind them to stock up around the holidays when people will be visiting.

3. Create frequent buyer programs.

4. Extend our line beyond just delivered water, to water-related items, and use them as premiums or market them through our own catalog. Our catalog could include items such as water pitchers, plant watering cans, pet dishes, travel mugs, and designer water coolers.

What other ways could we extend our line? We could market Fountain ice cubes, bagged and distributed in liquor stores and mini-markets. How about Fountain frozen pops in the freezer section of the grocery? Earthquake kits in California. Backpacking kits to outdoors people. What about coolers specially designed for recreational vehicles.

Okay, how many of these were on your list? How many targets did you think of that weren't on this list? Doesn't that prove, in almost any selection of potential target customers, the list could go on and on. But what's important to remember is, once you've established the image for your product, that image should be well-tended in *every* piece of advertising you distribute: A well-orchestrated advertising campaign springing from your core objective and positioning.

Are Your Tactics Strategic?
Is Your Strategy Tactical?

As general advertising and direct response embrace within their new/same advertising universe, they're going to have marry their children to each other, too. General advertising's child is "image." Direct response's child is "tactics." The offspring of this second union is the legitimate child of contemporary communication: an overall approach called "strategic marketing."

Advertising is too expensive—and too crucial to a company's health—to ignore that total family marriage any longer.

Marketing Checklist—Chapter 5

☐ 1. Does the sales argument in the coupon reinforce the sales argument in the ad? Or are the components unrelated?

☐ 2. Does the response device provide you with useful information about the respondent?

☐ 3. Does the response device avoid unexplained "shorthand" in the copy?

☐ 4. Does the response device tell the reader/viewer/listener what to do?

☐ 5. Does the response device clarify the specifics of the offer?

☐ 6. When using a bind-in response card with an adjacent space ad, does the space ad repeat the offer on the card?

☐ 7. Are you using both tabs of a bound-in card to direct the reader to your ad?

☐ 8. If you're looking for response to your ad, have you made it easy for your reader/viewer/listener to respond?

☐ 9. Once you've convinced a reader to respond, have you laid out a plan for continuing marketing dialogue with that respondent?

CHAPTER *6*

If It Isn't Direct, It Doesn't Follow Through

Every good marketer knows one surefire way to help turn "getting attention" into "getting a sale"—involvement.

Involve your readers. Spur them into action.

Figure 6-1 shows an interesting—and *involving*—twist on telemarketing: Get the customer to call *you* by using an integrated mix of print, outdoor advertising, and telemarketing.

Johnnie Walker Scotch ran this ad asking for a telephone response, first on outdoor boards and then in magazines.

The boards were first tested in California. Los Angeles was a good choice to test what was a revolutionary concept—the phone response outdoor board. In the crowded freeway system where commuters are often stuck in traffic for long periods, cars have become necessary extensions of the office. Car phones are very popular...almost universal. Billboards, subliminal in some locations, become primary when they break the monotony of staring at the taillights of the driver in front of you.

So it's not too surprising the Johnnie Walker outdoor boards

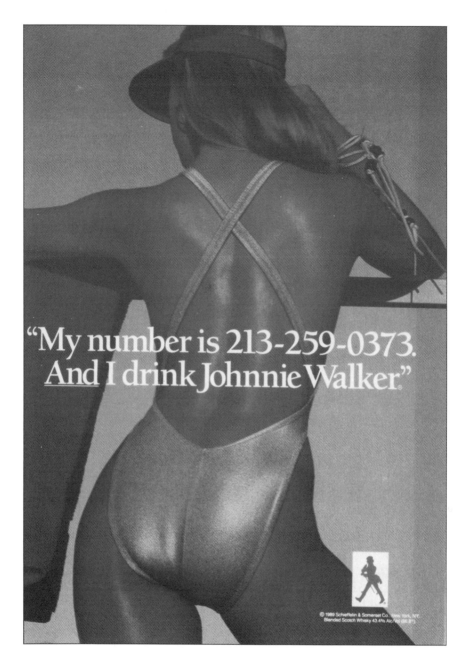

Figure 6-1

This ad was revolutionary in its mix of print, outdoor advertising and inbound telemarketing. But the recorded message is missing a sales motivator.

pulled in about 400 calls a day when the test campaign first broke on bill-boards around California.

Good idea. You take the attention you capture with the ads and turn it into action with a response phone number.

What kind of message does Johnnie Walker give to a caller? A tape re-cording of a female voice the other end of the line saying, "Hi. This is Su-san. I bet we have lots in common, especially if you drink Johnnie Walker. I like mine with diet cola on the rocks, especially the rocks overlooking Big Sur. I'm especially crazy about country rock, Tchaikovsky at the Holly-wood Bowl, rollerskating in Venice, and slam-dunking at the Forum. Thanks for calling. And remember, enjoy your Johnnie Walker. And please, for me, don't drink and drive."

That's it. That's the end of the recorded message.

Telemarketing or Tele-mix-up?

This advertiser went to a lot of trouble and expense to set up a phone call system that does what? It gives us a "radio" message over the tele-phone.

This message might have been included in the space ad with no dis-cernable difference—except in the cost to produce it.

But *would* it have had no discernable difference? Would the impact of even a non-message on an outdoor sign or a space ad be equivalent to the synergistic impact of sign plus phone?

One conclusion, regardless of advertiser or product: The telephone is a mighty weapon in the marketing wars of the 1990s, and any logical use in-creases the "Big 3"—Awareness, Image, and Sale. Without the phone, we have awareness only; and in the 1990s, awareness isn't enough.

If that's even partly true, what's missing here?

The tape-recorded message is missing a *sales* motivator. It doesn't make or even try to make a sale. That alone isn't a gaffe; but, when your ad is dynamic enough to induce somebody to call, it's criminal not to cap-ture a name and address for future proselytizing.

We can't attack the concept; we can question the execution.

Another New Twist in Adding Phone to Advertising

The advertisers liked this game so much, they decided to give it a new twist (figure 6-2). Here's my personal battle-report.

I faxed the number on the advertisement with this message: "So I drink Johnnie Walker Red. What about it?" I left only my fax number. No name. No address. I thought that would prompt them to ask for it.

Figure 6-3 is the company's faxed reply to my no-name fax.

Figure 6-2

Another new mix of outdoor advertising and inbound telemarketing: The fax advertisement. The faxed message is shown in Figure 6-3.

It's a cover sheet and a personalized hand-written message from ''Jennifer.''

Or *is* it a personalized message from Jennifer?

Take a look at the cover sheet. It's obviously not the same pen used to write the note. So this is really nothing more than a sort of pre-recorded fax—just like the earlier telephone recording. It doesn't ask me for any information, so whoever received my fax knows nothing about me—except for my fax number.

These ads are effective in spurring the reader to action. But even though they prompt action on the part of the target, they don't follow through. When the dialogue with a responder is discontinued, the full potential (getting the sale and getting repeat customers) of direct marketing is cut short.

How effective is a campaign that sells a *method* instead of the *results* of that method? And how effective is an incomplete database with nothing more than impersonal fax numbers?

Integrated communication? Yes, because both conventional and direct figured in the marketing mix. Effective use of both? To a point...but without capturing a name, the advertiser can never know for sure.

But wait! Figure 6-4 is *another* Johnnie Walker print ad which appeared around the winter holidays. It's clever, showing two reindeer apparently carrying on a conversation. The reindeer dressed up in red ''sleigh-towing'' tack says to the other reindeer, ''It's only part-time. *But* I deliver Johnnie Walker.''

The next page shows the reindeer facing the reader saying, ''I'll deliver Johnnie Walker Red for you. Just call 1-800-243-3787.''

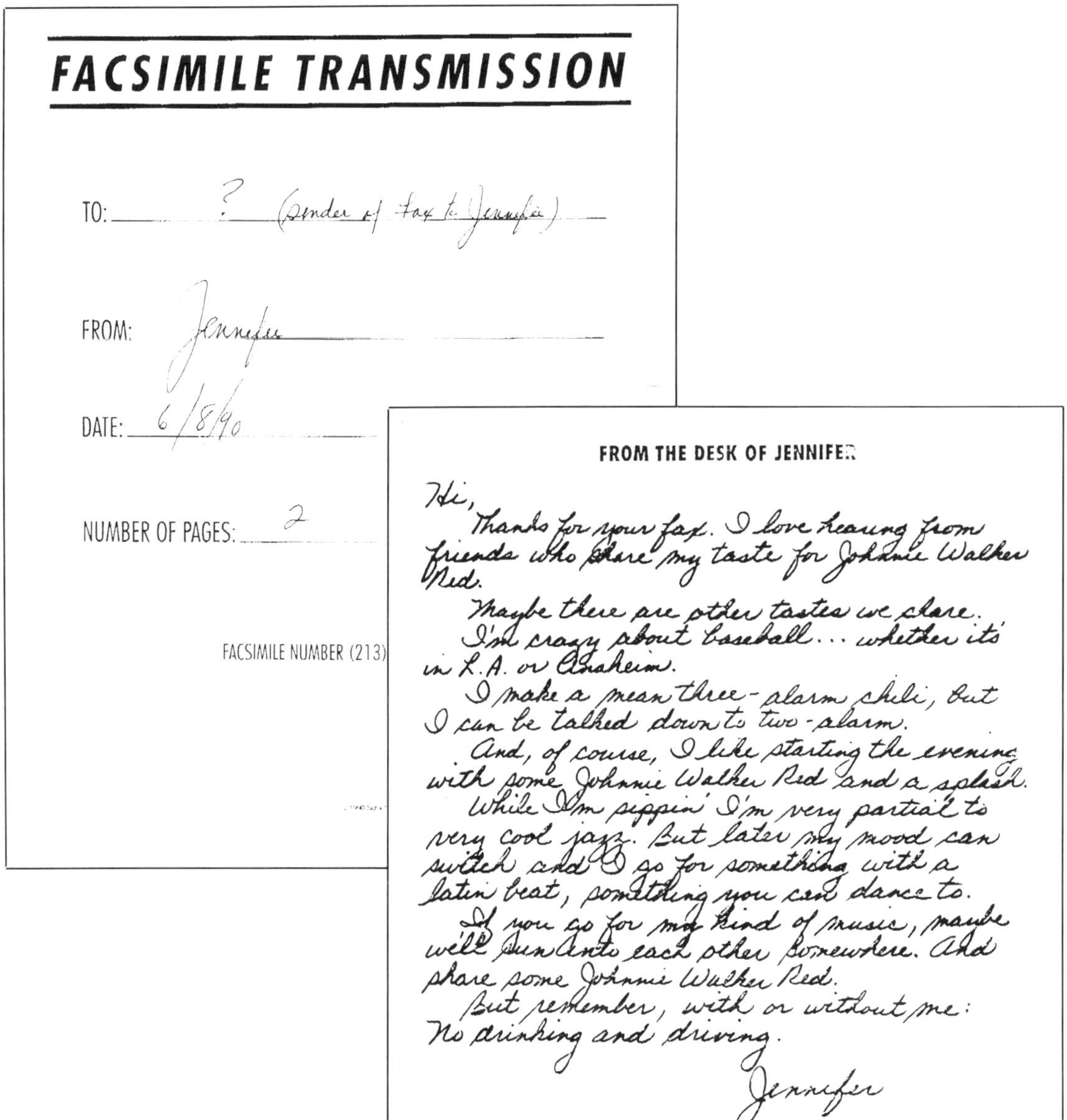

FACSIMILE TRANSMISSION

TO: _____?_____ (sender of fax to Jennifer)

FROM: Jennifer

DATE: 6/8/90

NUMBER OF PAGES: 2

FACSIMILE NUMBER (213)

FROM THE DESK OF JENNIFER

Hi,

Thanks for your fax. I love hearing from friends who share my taste for Johnnie Walker Red.

Maybe there are other tastes we share. I'm crazy about baseball... whether it's in L.A. or Anaheim.

I make a mean three-alarm chili, but I can be talked down to two-alarm.

And, of course, I like starting the evening with some Johnnie Walker Red and a splash.

While I'm sippin' I'm very partial to very cool jazz. But later my mood can switch and I go for something with a latin beat, something you can dance to.

If you go for my kind of music, maybe we'll run into each other somewhere. And share some Johnnie Walker Red.

But remember, with or without me: No drinking and driving.

Jennifer

JOHNNIE WALKER
ESTABLISHED 1820

Figure 6-3

Rather than a personalized message from Jennifer, the fax recipient receives a "pre-recorded" fax. The advertiser still has almost no information about who responded to this ad because the dialogue with the responder was cut short.

Figure 6-4

The phone number in this ad connects the caller to a live operator who makes it easy for the caller to buy this product immediately.

When we call the phone number in this ad we're connected with a live operator ready to take our order. Here's the true marriage of conventional advertising and direct response: Brand image isn't sacrificed for the order request, the order request isn't buried in an indecipherable copy block, and the advertiser doesn't let any grass grow on the customer's buying urge—a live operator makes it easy to buy right now.

> Keeping score by the number of times the phone rings without a sale *can't* parallel keeping score by the number of times the cash register rings.

The benefit of the marriage between the two facets of advertising doesn't change from chapter to chapter. Conventional lines up the target. Direct drills them between the eyes.

How Many Different Media Do We Need to Give 'em the Message?

Every day, on my way to the creative salt mine, I see another billboard. The cryptic message reads, "Your rent costs a lot. Checking doesn't have to."

My reaction: "Come again?"

Eventually, I see a TV commercial that *semi*-clears the mud in that comparison. In thirty frantic seconds, I'm told how many things in my life cost a lot; but, my checking account doesn't have to, because it's free (as long as I bank at this particular bank and qualify in a lot of different ways).

But how about those who haven't seen the TV commercials? Their comprehension is still coated with mud, because even if they understand the message—which they can, after driving past the board enough times—they face a non sequitur: Is the comparison to high rent a logical argument for free checking?

The problem is a common one in "conventional" advertising: One statement doesn't logically follow the other.

And the message on the billboard doesn't stand alone as a sales message without explanation in another medium.

How effective is a campaign that needs several different media to complete one sales message?

Is this "integrated communication," with one medium back up another? Or crap-game, with one medium *dependent* on another?

We Dare You to Decipher This Ad

Figure 6-5 is a full-page, 4-color magazine ad which reads: "Any Car, Any Day $29.95."

The illustration: A large bucket of water.

My reaction: "Huh?"

I spend some time squinting at the water bucket and am just able to make out a teeny drop of water rippling on the surface. Oh, I get the joke.

Figure 6-5

The ad is a visual pun. Will the casual reader flipping high-speed through this in-flight magazine take the time to figure it out?

It's a visual pun: The price of the car is just a drop in the bucket. (Ugh.) But a drop in the bucket compared to what? It doesn't follow, so I wonder —is my conclusion anywhere near what the writer actually is trying to transmit? For that matter, *is* the writer trying to transmit a message or to have everyone in the office cry, "How clever you are"?

And I find myself wondering just how many people flipping through this magazine will take the time to figure out the what and the why of this non-message. I suspect there must be a TV commercial out there to explain it.

Of course, when we really try to decipher this ad we eventually get the message. But how many "average consumers" (whose exposure to a thousand or more advertising messages every day desensitizes them to tough-to-comprehend visual cunning) will make the effort? As we're speeding down the highway or flipping high-speed through a magazine, how much time will we spend with an advertisement if we don't get a clear benefit right up front?

How effective is a sales message that uses non sequitur to sell?

> The assumption that a casual reader, listener, or viewer will regard an obscure or unclear advertising message as a challenge—and take the time to decode it, without becoming annoyed—is naive, unprofessional, and inevitably wasteful compared with a clear message, however primitive.

Infiniti jumped on the direct response bandwagon when they added a toll-free 800 telephone number to their television commercials. Considering *no one* is going to order a new car over the phone, we might ask, "What's the logic in this?"

The logic is there for us, all right: Getting people to call a toll-free number is a fast way for the car manufacturer to get sales materials into a prospect's hands. And a good way to collect the names of prospects interested in their cars.

I called the toll-free number and gently suggested to the woman who answered (and who had no idea *why* I was calling) she might take my address and send me some information on the car I had just seen in the ad.

Weeks later, I received an expensive mailing which included a dealer brochure. All headlines except the cover were written in Japanese characters. The cover headline read:

Q45
THE BEAUTY OF NATURE IS THAT
M30

Okay, none of those headlines told me anything. But the mailing also included a nice letter explaining the "philosophy" behind the product. ("It is a vision based on harmony. Tranquility. On a delicate balance between car and driver, between luxury and performance.") I was invited to visit my nearest dealer ". . . if you find this philosophy appealing."

I wasn't exactly sure what this "philosophy" had to do with buying a car, so I never called my dealer.

And I never heard from them again. Not surprising.

(So many ad writers think slapping an 800 phone number onto any ad makes it a direct response ad. Then when their illegitimate child dies in the marketplace, they tell their client, "See, I told you direct response doesn't work.")

What if, instead of just supplying a phone number (called for a non-message, as it turned out), they gave me a clear *incentive* to call—and

Figure 6-6

The components of this mailing work well together to give the reader an incentive right up front—but the offer is a blind cash inducement with no emotional image advertising behind it.

OU $50 TO MEET
EW LEADER

HEN SIT DOWN AT OUR BARGAINING TABLE AND FIND OUT HOW EASY SUMMIT IS TO OWN.

Once you have hands-on proof of Eagle Summit's outstanding ability to fulfill your driving expectations, we'll be happy to talk with you about making your relationship with Summit more permanent. Our sales-people will answer any questions you might have about Summit and its purchase or lease. You'll find the experience of owning a Summit easy to negotiate.

then followed through by having a professional salesperson on the line? What if, after several pages of muddy philosophy in the brochure, the call to action had prominently promised me a benefit if I responded? Wouldn't a well-orchestrated marketing effort tuned to the benefits of coming in and test-driving this car—rather than heavy reliance on lovely, but oblique metaphor—be worth the effort if it brought the customers to the sale floor (which a well-thought-out integrated marketing effort almost surely would)?

A competitive car manufacturer might be thinking along those same lines. Eagle mailed me an unsolicited coupon that promised to pay me $50 just to go in and test-drive a new Eagle Summit. The coupon and the accompanying brochure are figure 6-6.

Now here's direct response. The company offers a strong incentive, tightly tied to what they're trying to sell.

The brochure is in sync with the promotion itself. Not the standard informational brochure you find in a rack at the dealership (although it has useful information—and plenty of it), it's written around the promotion, hitting home the $50 I'll get if I simply walk into the dealership and test-drive the car.

Good benefit. Good promotion. Just two problems:

1. The sales pitch emphasizes I have to go to a *participating* dealer, yet doesn't give me an easy way to find one (short of going to the phone book and finding one myself). I might be willing to do that if I were aggressively in the market for this type of car. List technology is well beyond the ability to tie a specific dealer to a specific geographic location, so why didn't Eagle select a dealer for me. Recipient-response *isn't* as easy as the marketer might have made it.

2. The mailing came "cold." Advertising didn't set a climate for it, the way some of the more successful media-backed direct mail promotions have backed up their mailings. *Reader's Digest* and Publishers' Clearing House, for example, regularly reinforce their annual "blitzkrieg" mailing with a heavy television schedule so the mailing doesn't hit "cold." Eagle might have built an attitude of emotional receptivity through media advertising so the recipients weren't just following a blind cash inducement.

Why didn't they do this? One of three reasons:

1. Budget;
2. Ignorance;
3. Mailing to a selective *non-mass* group of targets, which would have made mass media advertising wasteful.

How One Marketer Integrated the Components

I'm coming to my point through a final example: a one-two punch that went to three—and worked every step of the way.

114

A department store where I have a charge card sent me a free sample of a product supposed to give me "clearer, more beautiful looking skin" (figure 6-7). Good benefit. Nice little present to find in my mailbox—how can I *not* notice it?

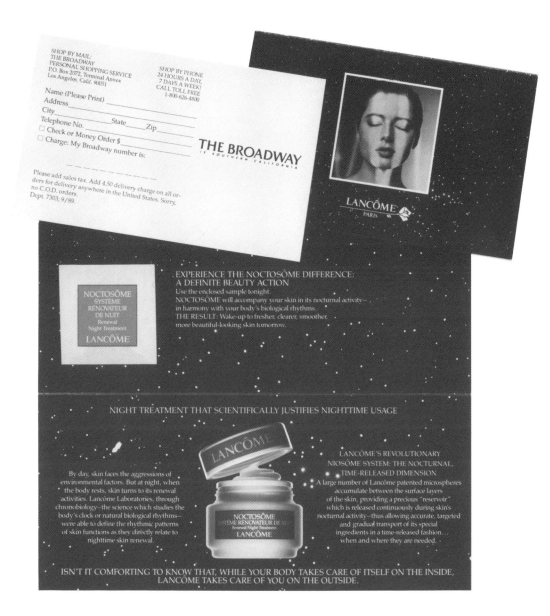

Figure 6-7

A free sample is a good way to hook your reader's attention—and get her to try your product.

115

Figure 6-8

In spite of the soft headline, this ad is noticed by the reader who received the mailing with the free sample (figure 6-7). Timing, benefit, and a well-orchestrated campaign transform an uninterested party into a live customer-prospect.

When you're fighting to grab target-attention and imagination fails you, a free offer is always a valid substitute. Human greed being such a prime motivator, "freebies" don't require imagination nor creativity; they're raw power on their own. In business-to-business promotions, free offers sometimes are the only way to crack the "secretarial barrier."

Exquisite timing! That evening, I opened a women's magazine and saw an ad (figure 6-8) I probably would have skipped over before, because of the weak, non-benefit oriented headline, "Lancome enters the world of Chrono-cosmetology." So what? But *now* I noticed the ad, because I'd just received a free sample of the same product and the promise of wonderful-looking skin. (The ad makes the same promise, but for some strange reason, not prominently.)

Later the same evening, a television commercial promised me beautiful-looking skin—again! A commercial for the same product—and *I stopped to pay attention to it*. If I hadn't been spurred by other stimuli, I might not have given that commercial, buried in a pod of five or six, a second glance.

One, two, three —knockout. I was transformed from an uninterested party to a live customer-prospect because of timing, benefit, and an ad campaign where each ad, although part of an entire campaign, stood on its own.

And that's my point. The most effective advertising campaigns use integrated, benefit oriented, targeted sales messages.

We don't have the communications world to ourselves. An integrated campaign combining *targeting* with *image*, tastefully and aggressively mounted, is a thing of beauty.

Marketing Checklist—Chapter 6

☐ 1. Do all the sales messages in your campaign reinforce the others— yet still stand alone as advertising messages? Or is each campaign component dependent on the other for its clarity and impact?

☐ 2. Does your advertising involve the message-recipient?

☐ 3. Have you honestly analyzed *who* your intended audience is? (Is it the prospective customer—or is it your peers within your office?)

☐ 4. Is your message instantly clear? Or are you making your reader/ viewer/listener work too hard to understand what you're trying to say?

☐ 6. Have you tied a strong incentive to what you're trying to sell?

CHAPTER 7

How You Can Combine Good Writing and Persuasive Writing While Your Competition Dies in the Trenches

Let's examine some examples of the holiest of marriages, between serviceable (technique) writing and persuasive (sales) writing.

When you decide to advertise a product, you declare war. Marketing war.

It's the kind of war we see on television when a bunch of musclebound louts climb into the ring as wrestlers. Last one on his feet is the winner.

Maybe your war doesn't get those banner headlines on the covers of the advertising trade magazines like the auto wars or cola wars do, but your war is just as serious, and in ratio of dollars-spent to ongoing enterprise, it's far more crucial. Lose, and your empire disintegrates.

Your crucial marketing war is on two fronts—the battle for every one of your paying customers and the battle to seize customers from another warrior. New competition springs up each year, like so many weeds in your garden. Those pesky weeds, who regard themselves as flowers and *you* as a weed, can choke off your growth.

The problem isn't new. You not only have to put a floor under the pulling power of every ad and every mailing, without increasing costs; but in a competitive marketplace, your perpetual aim should be to *boost* response. Standing still means you're falling backwards.

So your advertising has to be smarter, in two ways. One is finding new, more *persuasive* words and layouts to convince prospects to become your customers. The second is getting those customers to keep coming back.

Your Advertising: Muscle or Flab?

Take a look at your advertising. Examine the copy. Is it plain vanilla serviceable copy which doesn't do much more than describe what you have to sell? Or does your advertising push through your reader's built-up suspicions? Does your advertising just describe what you're selling? Or does it persuade the reader to buy—and to buy now?

Does your advertising serve as a clerk or a salesperson?

What's an easy, inexpensive way to revitalize your creative message? Sometimes all it takes is one black plate change at the printer: Rewrite your copy.

I'm really not being wry. Rewriting a so-so piece of copy before it appears in print beats the tar out of rewriting it after you've determined your advertising made no difference at all in your sales figures or (worse!) caused them to drop.

So take a good look at your copy and rewrite it if it doesn't involve your reader...if it doesn't speak to your reader personally and persuasively.

The difference between serviceable and persuasive copy is easy to see when you stop to look: Good basic copy gives the prospect *information* about the product you're selling. Persuasive sales copy either a) overpowers the prospect or b) makes the reader feel inferior unless he/she buys.

What a difference!

Any technical writer can inform. To get (and keep) customers, you have to be a powerful salesperson. The information you transmit has to grab and shake that reader so he or she can't help asking, "All right, where's my checkbook or Visa card?"

We writers *can* use copy to stack the deck in our favor.

How? A miracle surefire formula? I can do better than that, because any formula breeds sameness...which means you and your competitor could be mailing the same pitch.

Instead, I'll share with you some solid guidelines you can check your copy against, so you can be sure your next mail package or advertisement not only talks to your reader, but talks to your reader persuasively.

Universal Guidelines

These guidelines are universal. Check your copy against them—it doesn't matter if you're selling travel magazines, credit cards, or office supplies—and you can be confident you'll have a strong selling argument. (How can I be sure? Because I'm sure of the way people read.)

People expect us to talk to them personally. They expect us to talk to them about what *they* want. They expect us to give them a solution to *their* problems. That's why ego-driven ads can't pull as well as target-driven ads.

People expect completeness. That's why newspaper layout specialists end a front-page column and smart letter copywriters end the first page of a letter in mid-sentence. Readers demand a complete thought, so they'll turn the page to finish the message.

So, for starters, let's imagine ourselves out of our office, out from behind our keyboards. Let's place ourselves in the target's position of opening the newspaper, magazine, or mailbox and skimming through a bunch of ads or pulling out a bunch of envelopes. We're looking through the eye of the consumer. What catches his or her eye? Some copywriters believe if you present a question, your reader will automatically look for an answer.

We've seen too many mailings like figures 7-1 and 7-2.

Figure 7-1 says, "Will you please do us a favor?" Figure 7-2 says, "Will you do us a favor? (A favor that's bound to benefit you, too.)"

Figures 7-3 and 7-4 both are components of another mailing. Figure 7-3 is the carrier envelope. It gives us the answers (Yes/No/Maybe) before we know what the question is (figure 7-4).

And what is the question? Again, "Will you please do us a favor?"

The nerve of those questions!

We, as readers, know nothing about what's inside these envelopes—and the writer won't give us a reason to find out. The writer won't tell us up front how these envelopes relate to us, so we have no good reason to do any kind of favor for these people, much less open up their envelopes. These packages don't speak to us personally. All we have is a stranger asking for a favor—much the same way a beggar asks for a coin. But here's the difference between the beggar and these envelopes: The beggar is probably disheveled, and more than likely he looks like he needs a coin. Because he looks so forlorn, we might be inclined to help him out. These slick envelopes don't even give us that much motivation.

Ok, so let's modify that guideline a bit. Present an *interesting* question and your reader will automatically look for an answer.

This statement is true, but it doesn't give the kind of help a copywriter needs, if that copywriter is thinking like a salesperson. Who's to judge what's an ''interesting'' question?

Sometimes, interesting questions are universal.

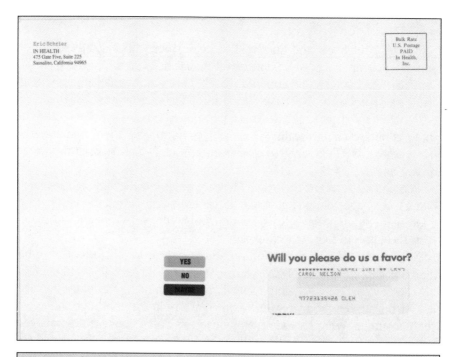

Figures 7-1 and 7-2

How many envelopes asking ''do us a favor'' does the average reader get every week?

Figures 7-3 and 7-4

This mailing gives us the answers first, and waits until we're inside be-
fore asking us for a favor.

Figure 7-5

The only people who could resist opening this envelope would be the ones who answer "no." And those people aren't the target audience here.

Figure 7-5, for instance. The headline reads, "Be honest. Could your love life be improved?" Through the window we see a "YES" and a "MAYBE" sticker. Who can resist opening this envelope? (You'll notice they haven't provided a sticker for a "NO" answer.)

A word of caution: Be careful when choosing an interesting teaser question. Writers struggle to find an interesting angle, and instead of landing in the reader's world of "interesting," their copy jumps head first into the sticky muck of "ridiculous."

Figure 7-6, I think we'll all agree, is a prime example of a ridiculous question. It says, "Can you tell if you're a man or woman (without looking)?" As you can see, it's multiple choice question—you answer yes, no, or maybe. (If your answer is no, you need a more basic education than this mailing can provide. For that matter, I wouldn't want to have dinner with anybody who answers, "Maybe.")

The envelope says, "The favor of a reply is requested." Which on its face makes it a ridiculous request. But it *does* get the reader to open the envelope—which is the prime function of envelope copy.

Let's look inside to see if we can shed some light on the question, "Can you tell if you're a man or a woman (without looking)?"

The first component we pull out is the reply card (figure 7-7). On the left-hand portion it says, "Free examination. No obligation."

So if you can't tell without looking, they'll look for you. In fact, they'll take a look for free.

The next component we pull out (figure 7-8) says, "If you don't believe us—look at what *U.S. News and World Report* has to say . . ."

Ah, so now they're hauling in the big guns to verify whether I'm a man or a woman. What more can there be? Do we dare read the letter?

124

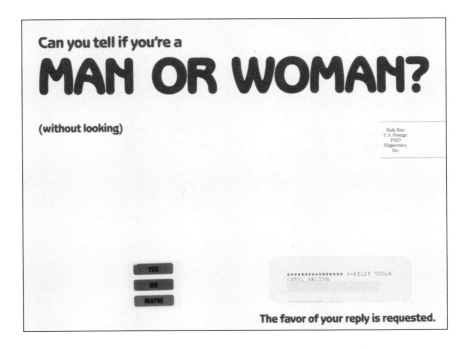

Figure 7-6

How many readers would answer "no" or "maybe" to this question?

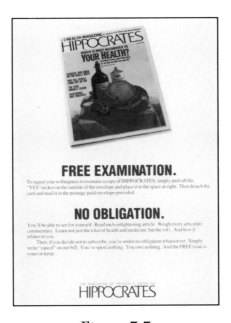

Figure 7-7

If the reader doesn't know the answer to the envelope's question in Figure 7-6 (without looking), he's entitled to an examination—free.

125

Figure 7-8

If the reader doesn't believe the "Free examination" results, he can defer to the opinion of U.S. News and World Report.

Figure 7-9

Does the reader bother to read on after this anti-climactic (and no-benefit) answer to the envelope's question?

In the letter (figure 7-9) the writer repeats the question. But here, at last, this marketer explains the difference between men and women in terms more likely to pique the interest of the prospective subscriber to this consumer-level medical magazine. It says, "If you're a man, your hands are usually warmer. Your face won't wrinkle as badly. You're less likely to be allergic to dogs and cats. And you have sexy little hairs on your ears."

"If you're a woman, you're not as prone to hay fever. Your eyes are less color-blind to red. Your senses of smell, taste, and hearing are much sharper. And your ears are as smooth as a baby's."

But so what? This is a classic example of a writer ignoring the magazine's benefits to the reader. And how much more effective the envelope copy would have been if it had hinted at useful and interesting information the reader can get from the publication. How much more effective it would have been with this no-brainer variation of the envelope teaser copy: "Can you tell if you're a man or woman? (Don't bother to look. We aren't talking about what you think we're talking about.)"

What can we ask our readers to get them to read our ad or open our package over our competition's? How do we determine what's the perfect question to ask?

Here's the answer, and it's so simple you can start using it thirty seconds from now:

Choose the right message for the right audience. Don't sit down at the keyboard to ask your readers a question until you've answered some questions you should have about *them*—about the people whom you're writing to. Don't write to them until you know them.

An example of this answer, in practice: Figure 7-10 is a mailing directed to advertising and marketing professionals. The publication they're selling is a magazine about consumer trends and lifestyles—a magazine designed to give advertising professionals information on American consumers.

The headline reads, "*Who* are the hottest new consumers? *What* do they want? *Where* are they?"

These questions are perfectly targeted to the audience at whom the magazine is aimed.

We know advertising executives received this mailing so we know the recipient of this package asks those same questions several times every day.

But the questions asked are vague and generalized, so the recipient may—or may not—be compelled to open the envelope.

Now let's compare the copy to another example from the same company, *American Demographics Magazine* (figure 7-11).

The provocative envelope uses effective child psychology. The headline on this envelope reads, "How well do *you* know consumers? A True/False quiz follows (who can resist a quiz?), inviting the reader to get involved with the piece.

The quiz has questions like: "Americans spend more on gambling than they donate to churches, True or False."

"A majority of Americans think they might have better sex if they had more money, True or False."

A small paragraph below the questions says, "If you think you know American consumers, answer these questions, look inside, prepare yourself for a shock—and send back this token for a FREE copy of the intriguing magazine that promises to tell you even more!"

The "shock" may be a mild one, but once the envelope is opened, mission accomplished!

The final hook: A die-cut window. Something is free inside.

Why do we assume the second package worked better than the first? One reason is my own "decoy" name got this mailing three times; the other mailing seemed to have died in its tracks. As far as I know, it went

Figure 7-10

These questions are well-targeted to the reader, but they're vague and generalized.

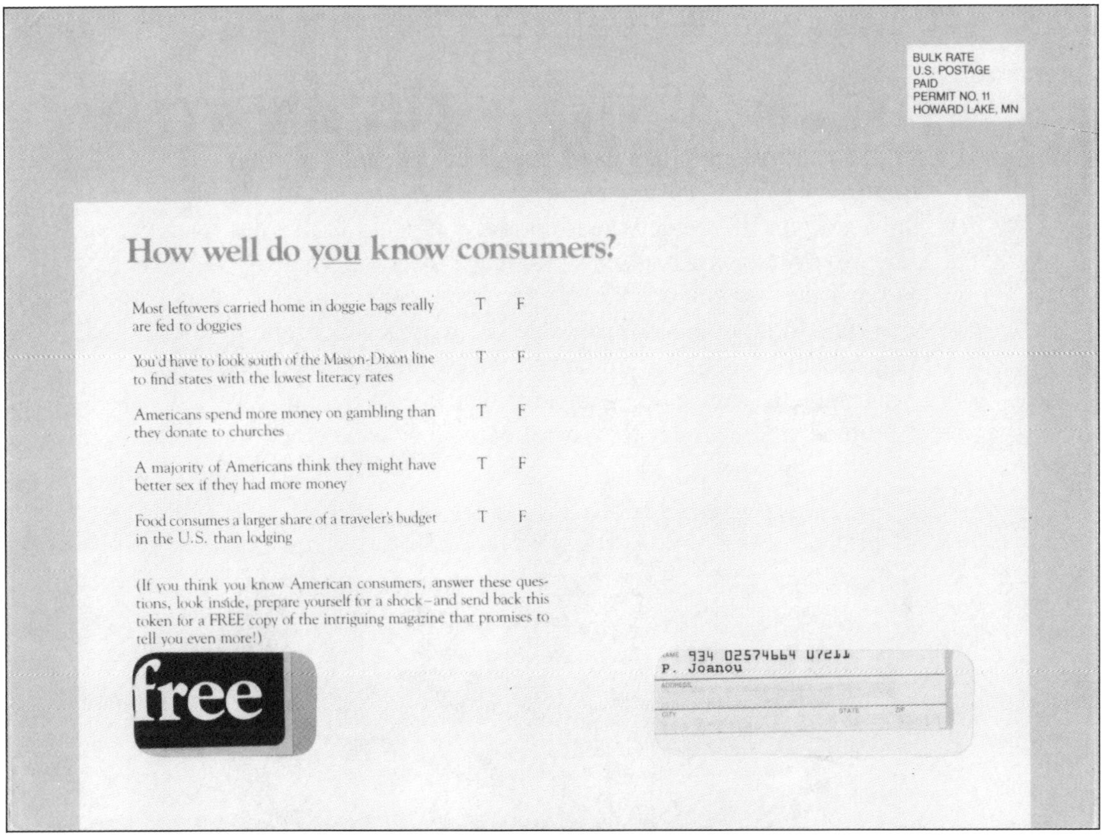

Figure 7-11

Specific questions on this envelope involve the reader.

out once and that was it. But even if we don't know the comparative results, we do know the writer not only climbs inside the head of the reader to pose the intriguing questions to the target audience; the writer persuades the reader to *get involved* with the sales piece.

How does the writer do this? With the simplest trick we writers have: specific questions that demand specific answers. The questions in the first package are vague and generalized. The reader doesn't really expect to find the answers to these questions inside the envelope. Instead, the reader expects to open the envelope to find a sales pitch.

And as a busy marketing executive, which envelope would have been more likely to induce you to take the time to read what's inside?

So let's revise our guideline one more time: Make the question provocative and your reader will look for the answer.

Follow this rule and you can't miss. And understand, please, this is just one road to success in writing envelope copy.

129

Whose Message Is It, Anyway?

Let's take a look at some catalog copy. Catalog copy by its very nature has to kill with one blow; and that blow should penetrate the reader's armor without damaging other descriptions in the same catalog.

When a woman buys a pair of pants, one important consideration weighs heavily in the buying decision: Do the pants flatter her figure?

Mail-order catalogs are at a disadvantage, since clothing has to be paid for and delivered before anyone can try it on. So how can catalogs convince anyone to buy a pair of pants before that person tries them on?

Many catalogs rely on photographs to show how clothing looks. But we veteran catalog-buyers all know by now that the fashion models they use are ten times more slender than most of us could ever hope (or want) to

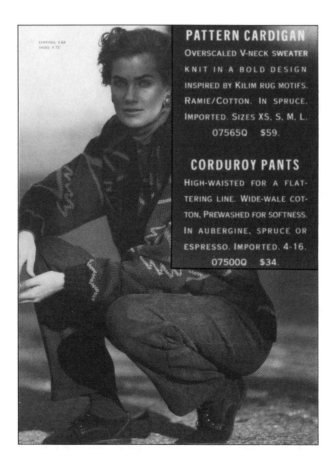

Figure 7-12

This catalog is short on copy—long on four-color photos (even though the photos semi-obscure what the pants actually look like).

130

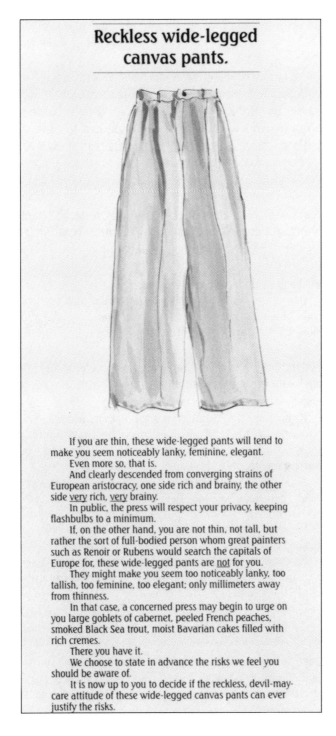

Reckless wide-legged canvas pants.

If you are thin, these wide-legged pants will tend to make you seem noticeably lanky, feminine, elegant.

Even more so, that is.

And clearly descended from converging strains of European aristocracy, one side rich and brainy, the other side <u>very</u> rich, <u>very</u> brainy.

In public, the press will respect your privacy, keeping flashbulbs to a minimum.

If, on the other hand, you are not thin, not tall, but rather the sort of full-bodied person whom great painters such as Renoir or Rubens would search the capitals of Europe for, these wide-legged pants are <u>not</u> for you.

They might make you seem too noticeably lanky, too tallish, too feminine, too elegant; only millimeters away from thinness.

In that case, a concerned press may begin to urge on you large goblets of cabernet, peeled French peaches, smoked Black Sea trout, moist Bavarian cakes filled with rich cremes.

There you have it.

We choose to state in advance the risks we feel you should be aware of.

It is now up to you to decide if the reckless, devil-may-care attitude of these wide-legged canvas pants can ever justify the risks.

Figure 7-13

Long on copy: Copy that turns the features of the product into reader-benefits.

be. We could search the entire world and not find one article of clothing that doesn't look good on these professional catalog models. So maybe the description needs a little sales-kicker.

That's where copywriter-salesmanship comes in. Figure 7-12 is a catalog photograph and written description of a pair of pants. The pants look perfectly wonderful on the model. We can see they're wide-legged, but the photo obscures the waistline. So the copy has to describe them to show us what's missing—and add a little punch to the sell:

CORDUROY PANTS. High waisted for a flattering line.

It then describes the material, colors and price of the pants.

Now let's look at figure 7-13, a page from another catalog. They're also selling high-waisted pants. Their copy reads:

Reckless wide-legged canvas pants.
    If you are thin, these wide-legged pants will tend to make you seem noticeably lanky, feminine, elegant. Even more so, that is.

Okay, good benefit for a thin woman. What about the women who aren't so thin? The copy continues...

If, on the other hand, you are not thin, not tall, but rather the sort of full-bodied person whom great painters such as Renoir or Rubens would search the capitals of Europe for, these wide-legged pants are not for you.
    They might make you seem too noticeably lanky, too tallish, too feminine, too elegant; only millimeters away from thinness.
    We choose to state in advance the risks we feel you should be aware of.
    It is now up to you to decide if the reckless, devil-may-care attitude of these wide-legged canvas pants can ever justify the risks.

Now here's a copywriter who knows how to change product features into product benefits. A copywriter who knows how to sell a pair of pants—because, of course, it's impossible for a not-so-thin woman to be "too noticeably lanky, too tallish" in the way she looks at herself. A classic case of the-grass-is-always-greener, it's what she's wanted all her life.

Talk about versatile copy!

And take a look at the picture. No photos of skinny models here, just a loose illustration of the pants.

I wonder what would happen if we combined this great benefit-oriented copy with *photorealism*, 4-color photographs of the clothes (no models,

Figure 7-14

What prompts a veteran catalog buyer to pay $146 for a $44 plumber's bag? The answer might be: Well-written, benefit-oriented, personal copy.

please, since *any* model shown wearing the pants would destroy the lovely image the copywriter conjures up in the reader's mind). We could be onto the formula for sales explosions.

Another example: What prompts a veteran catalog buyer to pay $146 for a $44 plumber's bag? The answer might be: Well-written, benefit-oriented, *personal* copy.

The persuasive copy in Figure 7-14 reads:

My search for something small enough to throw under
the airplane seat, but big enough to hold the ridiculous

> amount of stuff you actually need with you for meetings
> around town, or across the country, led me to discover
> the obscure but noble American plumber's bag.
>
> Slightly dashing, without trying too hard. And just
> enough different from everything else.

I know someone who bought the bag from this catalog (see, this *isn't*
just theory I'm talking about here—this stuff *does* work).

Also, I know it's available in my local hardware store for $44 (so it's not
so "obscure" after all). But you can bet, after reading this copy, I look at
this hardware-store plumber's bag in a different light.

The Danger of "Me"-Driven Copy

Take a look at figure 7-15. What do you think this ad is trying to sell?

Most people will think this ad is selling shoes. They'll get this idea from
the illustration used in the ad.

Are you surprised to find out this ad is introducing a new airline service?

The tiny white-on-black copy says, "July 18, 1950, 4:20 a.m. At the
Stonefield Maternity Home in Blackheath, South London. . .a child is
born. He seems to be smiling. At the exact same moment, in another part
of London. . .a top airline executive suddenly develops an inexplicable
nervous twitch. Coincidence? We don't think so. Introducing Virgin Atlantic Airways. . ."

Copy goes on to say the twitching airline executive now sells shoes in
Liverpool.

Ok, this is all in good fun. But let's look at what the advertiser did here.
He bought a full page newspaper ad. $55,000 for one day. He wrote "me"
driven copy—and he's not that good a storyteller. Because of that, we
may never get to what he's really selling here. And I don't have to tell you
how much trouble the airlines are in these days—it's absolutely cutthroat.
In that kind of advertising climate, how can anyone justify introducing a
new airline service with ho-hum, "me"-driven, muddy, unclear advertising?

And I don't know how to justify an ad in an American publication, written in French—ever (figure 7-16). But we seem to have a lot of it these
days. This one sells perfume, and in a perverse way I do understand what
this marketer is trying to do. It's pure snob appeal. But how many women
are scared off because the advertiser says, "I know something you
don't"?

Solution? As an opinion, a snob-appeal message written in highfalutin
English with an occasional *common* French word, like *oui* or *non* or *c'est
magnifique*.

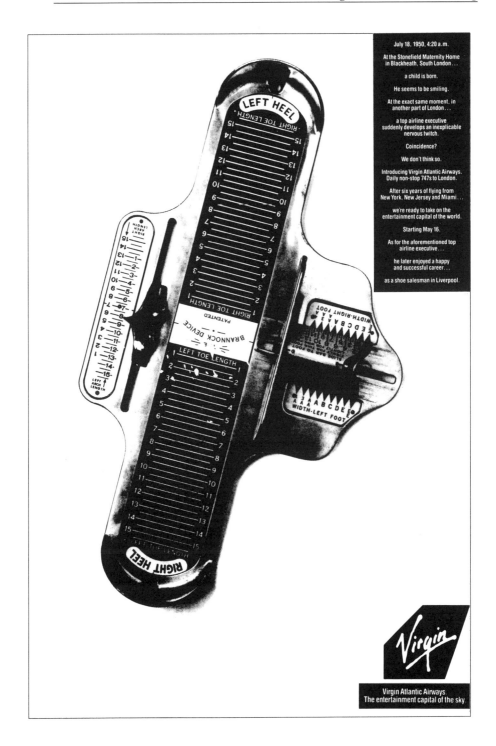

Figure 7-15

Quick! What's this ad selling? A classic example of "me" driven copy.

To a Salesperson, the Future Is NOW

Too often the person who writes or designs an ad or a mailer and the person who produces it aren't spending their own money.

I'd bet this week's lottery jackpot these people wouldn't justify "long-range image-building and we'll get to hard sales later" if their own money was on the line. They aren't thinking as marketers because they don't have to.

Divorcing image-building from salesmanship is a powerful step backward. In the 1990s our marriage is more than one of convenience; it's one

Figure 7-16

French copy translates to pure snob-appeal. But how many readers are scared off because the advertiser is saying "I know something you don't"?

136

of necessity, because our children—the messages we pour out of our word/art machines—have to find happy homes with those target-people out there.

So we give our prospect a reason to respond now. *Now* while the buying urge is hot. That means a limited time offer. A premium that's in short supply. A gift to the first 100 responders—anything—to make sure they respond before they forget about it.

Our job is to be communicators. Our job is to be marketers. Our job is to sell.

Still not convinced? Then I hope you're my competitor.

Marketing Checklist—Chapter 7

☐ 1. Have you combed through your copy and replaced ordinary, merely descriptive (clerk) language with active, *persuasive* (salesperson) language?

☐ 2. Have you spiced up your information with compelling reasons to buy?

☐ 3. Have you scrutinized what your customers want? Have you answered every major question they might ask about why they should buy?

☐ 4. Have you teased your readers with provocative questions which demand specific answers they can get only by opening the envelope?

☐ 5. Have you presented your product features as product benefits?

☐ 6. Is your copy "you"-driven? Or is it pompously "me"-driven?

☐ 7. Have you established reader-rapport? Or have you inadvertently scared off your readers by hinting you know something they don't?

☐ 8. Have you given your prospect a reason to respond *now*?

CHAPTER *8*

Enlightened Direct Marketing: Problem-Solving and New Techniques

We're approaching the twenty-first century with a rapidly-developing set of new tools. Our tools are rhetorical, the result of a *different* awareness—awareness of how valuable the inter-relationship of conventional advertising and direct marketing can be.

One rhetorical tool: When writing an advertising message, put your arms around the reader; embrace the reader. Arm's length copy will rarely bring the reader close enough to let you sell anything.

Get to know why someone would be interested in buying your product—and then write about it in a way that appeals to that reader.

That means choosing a message calculated to appeal to your audience, not to the folks in your office.

Let's explore a few avenues leading us to increased response.

If They Don't Open It They Won't Read It

Anyone who has been in the direct mail business for more than twenty minutes knows a ghastly truth: If the recipient doesn't open the envelope, no amount of brilliance inside that envelope has any significance at all.

How do we tempt our customer to read our tiny ad or open our envelope? This could be a problem, unless we 1) use our new-found creative problem-solving, and 2) write interesting headlines and/or provocative teaser copy.

Figure 8-1 is an envelope that arrived in February—just about the time everyone is preparing to pay income taxes. It says, ''Confessions of a former IRS agent.''

Ah! Inside poop from a former agent of the most feared bureau in the whole government—the Internal Revenue Service. Imagine ''Confessions of a former IRS agent'' as the headline of an ad in the February issue of a magazine. It would work just as well because it's interesting enough to get you to read the body copy.

The particular envelope shown in figure 8-1 is torn. No surprise, because you can bet whoever received this mailing tore it open to get at the contents. The envelope teaser copy implies the envelope holds some secret information about the dreaded ''Big Brother'' and how he uses his microscope on our tax returns.

Power lies in two little words. The first word is ''confessions.'' That word implies something never before revealed to the outside world . . . something the former IRS agent is baring his soul about.

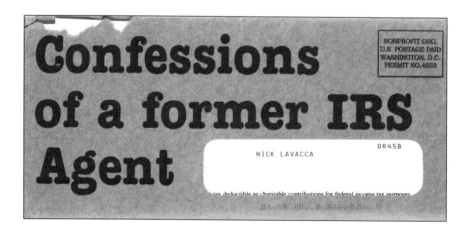

Figure 8-1

Powerful envelope copy. Not surprisingly, this envelope is torn—the reader tore it open in a hurry to get at the contents.

Figure 8-2

The envelope promises useful information to the traveler who receives this mailing.

The second word is "IRS," but power actually comes from "IRS" *plus* the words around it. The word before IRS, "former," and the following word, "agent" imply the message is from a member of a secret clan who no longer has to honor a vow of secrecy.

The recipient of this mailing interprets envelope copy the way the writer wants him to interpret it—he'll get access to secrets he really isn't supposed to have, from someone who used to be on the inside.

The envelope was unbleached brown paper. Clever! It not only is inexpensive, significant if we're on a tight budget, but it's also a good choice for the message. Why? Because a "brown paper wrapper" underscores the point: You're getting something undercover—something in secret.

What kind of format would you use to give the impression of "secret information" if you were using this as a space ad? You could use an "advertorial" or "reader" format. This makes the information in the ad look as though it's part of the magazine's editorial; there only for the readers of this magazine.

Figure 8-2 is a package mailed to travelers. Travelers who fly. Travelers who, more than likely, feel jet lag. Many of those travelers have heard or read the reason for jet lag might be what they eat while they're traveling. So the big, bold headline, "What never to eat on an airplane," promises useful information to the reader of this package. And we can bet it was opened. (Again, you could accomplish the same interest in a space ad by using the same headline in an advertorial placed in an in-flight magazine ...if an in-flight magazine accepts the ad.)

The envelope shown in figure 8-3 says, "Tap. Taptap. Taptaptap. Taptap. (decoded inside)"

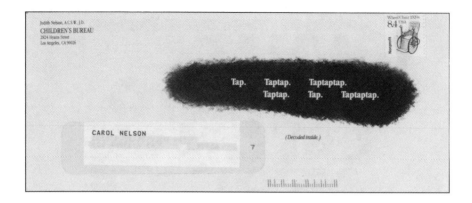

Figure 8-3

An engaging envelope hook to get the reader to see what's inside.

And what's inside? The translation: "Taptap: are you still there? Tap. Tap. Yes, we're still ok."

The letter tells about two orphaned brothers whose secret code is tapped on the wall between their bedrooms every night. It's an engaging hook to get you to read the letter.

The Letter: Foundation of Direct Mail

Now we come to the letter. The letter is strictly the domain of direct mail. A letter is personalized to the recipient of the package, just as a letter from your best friend would be.

But here's the difference: A sales letter *isn't* from your prospect's best friend. In fact, because your prospect has been preconditioned (by a history of receiving bad, formula-driven sales letters), unless you grab the reader's attention right away, your sales letter may end up in the trash before the salutation is read.

Do you know the difference between good letter copy and *persuasive* letter copy? Including solid information about your product is important, but how can you write a persuasive letter to transform your "ho-hum" advertising message into a top-notch sales vehicle?

For any successful direct market letter, we do have some helpful rules to follow. I prefer to call these rules "guidelines." Why? Because if you don't think of them as just guidelines, you're apt to fall into the "technique trap." That is, writing a letter that follows the rules—but which doesn't have any soul.

Worship of "technique" has been the downfall of many a direct response writer. Here's where adherence to the principles of *image* advertising can help. The marriage between conventional advertising and direct marketing has dowries both ways.

Lots of letter-writing books before this one concentrate (safely) on letter-writing technique.

These experts—and they *are* experts—share what I call "construction details."

They tell you what a "Johnson Box" is. (I won't, because I think a Johnson Box is implicitly weak.) They tell you where to position an overline. They tell you why you should use a p.s. They describe optimum paragraph length. They tell you where to introduce the offer and where to repeat it. They tell you how long the letter should be—one page for business-to-business, two pages for financial offers, four or six pages for subscriptions, up to sixteen pages for newsletters.

There's something aggravating about the "technique letter." If you follow standard direct mail letter "technique" slavishly—even if your content is *all* technique, without any soul—chances are your letter won't fail. It probably will get some response if you have a good offer and mail to targeted lists.

And response depends in part on what your competition is mailing at the same time. If your competition has a better written message, and they go to the same lists with the same offer, they're likely to blow you right out of the water.

I said there's something aggravating about the "technique letter." My objection is based partly on the sour realization that such a letter *will* generate some response. But my primary gripe is aimed at the writer, who becomes a technician instead of a communicator. The writer regurgitates facts according to a pre-set grid. Anybody—anybody—who ever has sold shoes in a retail store knows that a competent clerk never can achieve the sales volume an instinctive salesperson can.

So when we pay more attention to how to write a letter rather than what's in the letter, we settle for results that just have to be poorer than we might have had.

Let's look at some letters to see how two writers approached the same message.

The first letter's overline (figure 8-4) reads, "A FREE no-obligation opportunity to discover the profitable advantages of AMERICAN DEMO-GRAPHICS, The Magazine of Consumer Markets."

We might—if we tried hard—think of a less inviting overline. What's the offer here? A free opportunity. Gee, you mean I don't have to pay for this

```
American
Demographics

                                           A publication of Dow Jones & Company, Inc.
                                          Publishers of The Wall Street Journal and Barron's


              A FREE, no-obligation opportunity to discover the
              profitable advantages of AMERICAN DEMOGRAPHICS,
                    The Magazine of Consumer Markets.

    Dear Business Professional:

          Do you want to keep on top of your customers' changing buying
    habits and your shifting markets?

          Do you want to avoid wasting hundreds of hours of work and
    thousands of dollars...missing profitable opportunities...and
    becoming ''obsolete''?

          If you sell to the American consumer...if you make decisions
    affecting your company's marketing, advertising, or sales
    strategies...if you're responsible for developing new consumer
    products or services...if you're in advertising or the media...

          —AMERICAN DEMOGRAPHICS will give you vital information and
    insights you need. To revamp plans and products to be more
    profitable today and reach your new and changing customers to
    ensure your successful future.

          With AMERICAN DEMOGRAPHICS, you'll have a clearer and more
    accurate view of WHO your new customers are...WHAT they want to
    buy...WHERE they are now and where they are going...HOW MUCH money
    they have to spend...and HOW you can sell them.
```

Figure 8-4

Can we think of a less inviting overline than the one on this letter?

opportunity? Thank you very much. This overline proves that no matter how poor we think our writing is, somebody else writes worse than we do.

How does the other package handle the overline (figure 8-5)?

You remember the envelope asked the recipient some questions (figure 7-11). This overline poses another question, ''Why do people buy what they buy?'' And right away it satisfies our demand for completion by giving us the answer: ''Two reasons . . . to get what they don't have—and to keep what they've got . . . but if that's not quite enough; if you still have a few questions about who, what, where, when and what price; you should get to know the lively authoritative magazine that fills in these details. It's called American Demographics . . . and this is your chance to get the next issue FREE!''

I grant you this overline is brutal, because it's far too long. But we're discussing communication, not technique. What's the difference in copy here? The first overline imparts dry, uninviting semi-information. It uses such nonsense phrases as ''profitable advantages,'' when it should be telling us *(Don't write to them until you know them)* what those profitable advantages are. And the one glaring unasked question—why should I the reader be interested?—is also glaringly unanswered.

On the other hand, the second communication begins a dialogue between the writer and the reader. It's far from perfect. In fact, the point it makes is obvious, and the writer uses far too many words to make it. But it *is* aimed at the reader.

Gather the Reader into Your Arms

Two more examples from the murderously competitive world of magazine publishing. The first example doesn't gather the reader inside the magazine's arms. The second does.

Figure 8-6 is the front and back of a big nine by twelve inch glossy self-mailer for a travel magazine. The copy is somewhat weak, because it's generalized. It reads, "In every issue / Lively articles on vacation places in the U.S. and Canada...Handy detailed maps...little-known places

American Demographics

Why do people buy what they buy?

Two reasons, according to one marketing guru:
"To get what they don't have -- and to keep
what they've got."

There you have it.

But if that's not quite enough; if you still
have a few questions about who, what, where,
when and at what price; you should get to
know the lively, authoritative magazine that
fills in these details. It's called

American Demographics

... and this is your chance to get the next
issue FREE!

Dear Marketing Professional:

Exasperating, aren't they?

I'm talking about human beings. Americans. Consumers. The public.
The markets. The crazy-making jury out there you're paid to understand --
and whose whims and flights of fancy you're rewarded for predicting.

Just what do they want? And what will they want tomorrow?

My guess is that like most of us in this line of work, you could use all
the reliable help you can get -- not only in digging out the facts about what
really is going on, but what's likely to go on in the future.

Figure 8-5

This overline begins a dialogue between the writer and the reader with information aimed at the reader.

Figure 8-6

Standard, clichéd travel copy doesn't pull the reader into the sales copy.
But the easy-order response card might boost response.

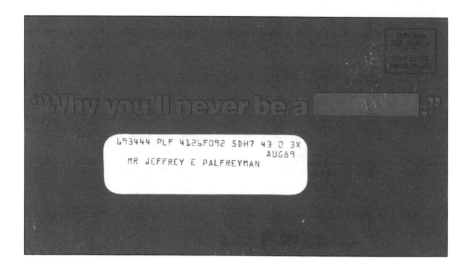

Figure 8-7

What reader can resist opening this envelope to find out what the completed sentence says?

within easy reach of your budget.'' Not very exciting to any experienced traveler. And travelers have to be the targets of this mailing.

Standard stuff: Pretty pictures and a free trial issue offer. The reply card is easy to send back, so an uninterested recipient might mail it just to get a free pretty magazine to show off on the coffee table.

Figure 8-7 shows a smaller package—measuring just four by seven and a half inches—for another travel magazine. The copy reads, ''Why you'll never be a...'' A what? A large bar blocks out the last word of the sentence. Our demand for completeness compels us to open the envelope.

Inside the package (figure 8-8), the top of the letter fills in the blank for us. It says, ''Why you'll never be a *tourist*.''

At first glance that's a strange thing for a travel magazine to say. Aren't they writing to tourists?

No, not this magazine. They know their primary audience is the person who researches a destination and finds the little hideaways that most others never know about. These people, and others who want to be thought of as ''in-the-know,'' are the targets. Ordinary tourists would have little motivation to buy this publication.

So the slant on this magazine is inside information not readily available to just anyone.

How do they approach the sales message to their readers? By underscoring the distinction between two simple words: Tourist vs. Traveler.

Choosing individual words is why copywriters exist. The word difference doesn't seem to be a great one—the difference between ''tourist'' and ''traveler''...until we read on.

A huge copy-block precedes the body of the letter:

> Every tourist wants to be a traveler. The traveler gets the room with the view; the tourist is still being driven from the airport the long way around. The tourist books into a New England hideaway next to construction crews building a mall. The traveler soaks up the sun in a deserted cove that will cost next to nothing; the tourist can barely find a place to sit on the crowded beach that costs so much more...

We've all been the tourist in this copy. It really strikes home. And even though the mailing shown in figure 8-6 has glossy pictures, if we have a choice, who would ''journey to little-known places within easy reach of our budget,'' the nondescript destination of the first package, before we'd ''soak up the sun in a deserted cove that costs next to nothing,'' the targeted-at-us destination of the second package?

Every tourist wants to be a traveler. The traveler gets the room with the view; the tourist is still being driven from the airport the long way around. The tourist books into a New England hideaway next to construction crews building a mall. The traveler soaks up the sun in a deserted cove that costs next to nothing; the tourist can barely find a place to sit on the crowded beach that costs so much more...

```
Dear Traveler:

In the next few days, thousands of people who love
travel will receive the latest issue of Condé Nast
Traveler.

But even though you are a traveler, you won't be
among them.

In the next few months, these people will travel from
Singapore to Southampton.  From Cannes to Canton.
Florence to Fiji.  Montserrat to Montana.  New Mexico
to New South Wales.
```

Figure 8-8

The letter completes the sentence—and aims its sales message at the target audience by drawing the distinction between the ''tourist'' and the ''traveler.''

See the status difference between the words tourist and traveler? This writer used targeted words to emphasize *exclusivity*. The language has been manipulated to make this package persuasive—and to get the prospect to identify with the product. How? By drawing the distinction between those two little words.

Big Ideas Can Beat Big Budgets

If we arm ourselves with the power of thoughtful, persuasive copy, we don't need huge budgets. We don't always need glossy photos or jumbo packages.

If that first copywriter/art director team had developed a well-thought-out sales argument, how much more effective those glossy photos would be! Imagine combining the easy-to-respond format of the first package with the persuasive sales copy of the second package. You could be generating sales dynamite.

Take another look at figure 8-8. The writer has established a ''tone-of-voice'' for the letter and is speaking to the reader personally.

> Dear Traveler [remember, they've already distinguished the traveler from the tourist in the overline, so the reader is already primed to be addressed as a ''traveler''],
>
> In the next few days, thousands of people who love travel will receive the latest issue of Condé Nast Traveler. But even though you are a traveler, you won't be among them.

Notice the switched gears. Seconds ago, the reader was part of an exclusive inside group. Now the reader is left behind—no longer part of this ''in'' group. This is a tricky switch. And here it *almost* works. Except for one word. Which one?

''Thousands.''

The writer started to forge a path of exclusivity in the letter by setting the reader apart from the herd. Now he's telling the reader, ''You won't be lumped with thousands,'' which the reader might well think is *good*. ''Thousands'' is about as exclusive as being in the phone book.

The first sentence would have worked better—the reader wouldn't have simultaneously felt like part of the herd and left out of the ''in'' group—if that one word had been left out of the sentence altogether or replaced with ''a select group.''

Does this seem like a minor point? Our business is *full* of minor points. Each minor one glues itself to others, which in bulk become *major*, either enhancing or damaging our daily sales figures.

> As a marketer, you want thousands of responses. As a communicator using exclusivity as a motivator, you'd better say to the reader, "Only you."

Always focus your attention on the reader—not yourself as the marketer, or, worse, as the writer. Don't write to see your own clever words on the page.

Write what the reader wants to read, not what *you* want to say. This is easy...and it isn't easy. It's easy because it's as logical as any rule of marketing can ever be. It isn't easy because it means locking both your ego and your desire to be clever in the closet until you've finished writing the package.

Does Your Target Know What You Know?

At this writing Sears and IBM have launched a major advertising campaign for Prodigy, their joint-venture interactive computer information system.

What is it?

Those familiar with services such as Compuserve know what it is. For others, Prodigy is a mystery.

Early television spots not only didn't solve the mystery, they compounded it. A quick snippet showed its use as an encyclopedia; another quick snippet showed its use as a stock market reporting service. Altogether, the campaign seemed structured by a conventional advertising agency, *showing* what it is instead of *explaining* what it is.

The difference? It's the difference between leaving out what the reader might want and generating the desire to buy. The television viewer or space ad reader wants to know, "What will it do for me?" So the 800 number has no motivator behind it.

A direct response integration would have made a change. The marketing team would have selected specific target after specific target, nailing each one individually.

One commercial might have had a youngster asking, "Dad, why don't we get an encyclopedia so I can look up the members of the Supreme Court I need for that classroom report?" The father answers, "We do have an encyclopedia. It's right on our computer monitor, and it's the best encyclopedia ever put together because it's updated every day."

Then *another* commercial might feature stock market reports. Each commercial becomes an arrow aimed at a specific, logical target.

The Formula Doesn't Change

Whether you're selling subscriptions or soap, automobiles or aardvarks, the formula doesn't change.

1. You write for the reader, not for your admirers in the office.

2. You stroke the reader without patronizing.

3. You tell the reader what's in it for him or her, not for you the marketer.

4. You subordinate the technical aspects of "how it works" to the emotional aspects of "what it does for *you*."

What an easy formula! But what a too-often ignored formula!

Take your reader by the hand and lead him/her through your sales argument. Combine good writing and persuasive writing. In fact, don't just combine them, scramble them to make them the most married, undivorceable couple in the world of 1990s marketing.

Marketing Checklist—Chapter 8

☐ 1. Have you put your arms around your reader in your copy? Or is your copy written at arm's-length?

☐ 2. Have you written your copy to appeal to your reader? Or to appeal to your own interests?

☐ 3. Are your envelope design and copy provocative enough to do the envelope's sole job—to get the recipient to open it?

☐ 4. Does your letter grab the reader's attention right off the bat?

☐ 5. Is your sales letter persuasive? Or does it worship at the shrine of technique, paying more attention to how the letter is written than what it says?

☐ 6. Does your sales letter begin a dialogue with the reader?

☐ 7. Have you made the reader feel selected?

☐ 8. Have you focused your words on the reader? Or do you write too much about yourself as the writer?

☐ 9. Have you told the reader what's in it for him/her?

CHAPTER *9*

Specialized Problem-Solving: Fund Raising, Public Relations, Retailing

Integrated marketing is more than ad writing.

Now we'll explore ways of bringing the reader into the fund raising writer's arms; establishing an individual or company as the voice of authority through public relations; and one of the most difficult problems, how retailers maintain market image while ringing up the cash register.

Bringing the Reader into the Fund Raising Writer's Arms

One of the most emotional segments of direct marketing is fund raising.

Fund raising has four conventional faces:

1. Direct mail
2. Telemarketing
3. Space and broadcast public service advertising
4. One-on-one confrontation.

Awareness plays a role in donor decisionmaking, which is why public relations should be—but too often isn't—a major factor in an organization's planning and budget.

Non-profit organizations which sacrifice attention to image because image doesn't result in direct dollars are taking the short view. Fund raising is a textbook example of the benefit of integrated marketing. Who would know or care about the Salvation Army or the Red Cross or UNICEF without an ongoing image-maintenance campaign?

> Fund raising does have the rare logic of celebrity use. A celebrity attracts news and feature coverage, and the charity benefits from the endorsement (even those endorsements which obviously are tortured and insincere—the result of a negotiation with the celebrity's agent).

The fund raising writer's daunting challenge: Convincing prospects to buy a promise—a promise to feed hungry children. . .a promise of a political candidate's intentions. . .a promise of a better world.

How does the writer sell a fund raising cause without giving anything concrete in return? Three ways:

1. By gathering up the reader into his arms.
2. By massaging the reader's ego.
3. By tapping into the reader's guilt.

The successful fund raising writer is one who does an emotionally convincing job of persuading both prior donors and cold prospects to support a cause that appeals to them. It isn't easy! Oh, sure, we all have causes that appeal to us *before* a fund raiser pitches us. Getting money from us for those causes doesn't require great talent. But response-oriented fund raisers know how to make a cause (about which our prior attitude was at best apathetic) appeal to us.

The Differences Between Various Lists of Names

In the past, fund raising mailings usually would split themselves between prior donors and logical cold list names. In the late 1980s, they split major donors and minor donors, and sometimes created yet another split based on the frequency of donations. Some add another split—donors recruited through broadcast appeals.

As we work our way into the database-driven 1990s we can anticipate still another split: The reason for giving.

I'll give you an illustration. Environmental fund raising groups such as Ducks Unlimited and Quail Unlimited find themselves in a 1990s quandary. Traditionally, they've written their appeals to hunters with the venerable battle cry, "Save the Wetlands" and "Save the Woodlands." The logical reason, if the dwindling wetlands and forest preserves disappear, ducks and quail disappear with them.

In the born-again environmental movement of the 1990s, "Save the Wetlands" can reach a lot more potential donors—non-hunting environmentalists as well as hunters.

Talk about different market groups! Obviously, we can't use the same appeal to both groups, because the reason for giving is entirely different. Yet it *is* possible to rally both groups around the same conservationist flag if we tailor our sales message to each group (figures 9-1 and 9-2).

Knowing the reason a donor gives to an organization is a copywriter's dream and a response-analyst's challenge. A copywriter's dream because the organization needs a multiplicity of appeals just to stand still and not fall backwards; a response analyst's challenge, because mounting a multiplicity of appeals is meaningless if we don't have the ability to tabulate the response and eliminate the losers.

Tailoring the Appeal: Credibility + Emotion

So how does the fund raising writer tailor those appeals to different prospect groups? By speaking to the reader personally—which translates to speaking to the reader *persuasively.*

For example, a fund raiser for runaway kids wrote what was to be a grabber plea for money:

> Since that night countless numbers of kids have knocked
> on that door...

The writer probably didn't know how many kids knocked on the door, so a specific reference to number of kids would have been an impossible copywriting task. Yet a specific number would lend credibility to the pitch.

So how might we change this phrase to make it seem like a specific number? We substitute "many thousands," or if it's more accurate, "many hundreds." Either of these two phrases *seems* to be a more specific number than "countless numbers."

The letter continues...

> ...we keep the doors open—open wide to give kids food,
> clothing and shelter. We can't turn away even one.

155

Why say "we *can't* turn away even one"—which implies we have no choice? We should say: "We *won't* turn away even one," or "We'll *never* turn away even one." Not only do the resolve and dedication to the cause become contagious, but "won't" reflects determination, while "can't" reflects lack of control.

How might we make the previous sentence more persuasive? This piece of copy doesn't need radical surgery—it just needs warmth.

> . . . we keep the doors open—open wide to give kids food, clothing, shelter—*life itself.*

What are we doing when we change this? We're reinforcing dedication and adding a touch of reader-guilt to the mix.

An effective fund raising appeal, like any effective advertising, involves the reader. It brings the reader into the writer's arms. So when this letter says, "you help give strength and meaning to a young life," it's good copy. But we can involve our reader even more by saying, "you literally restore strength and meaning to a young life."

And we continue to gather and hold the reader in our arms when we replace one word in the sentence, "We won't allow these lives to be thrown away."

You know by now what we change: *"You and I* won't allow these young lives to be thrown away."

What about signing this letter? We haven't gone to the trouble of gathering the reader into our arms only to push him back at the final moment.

Figure 9-1

This traditional Ducks Unlimited message is aimed at duck hunters. The silhouette photograph shows two hunters with a bird dog and decoys.

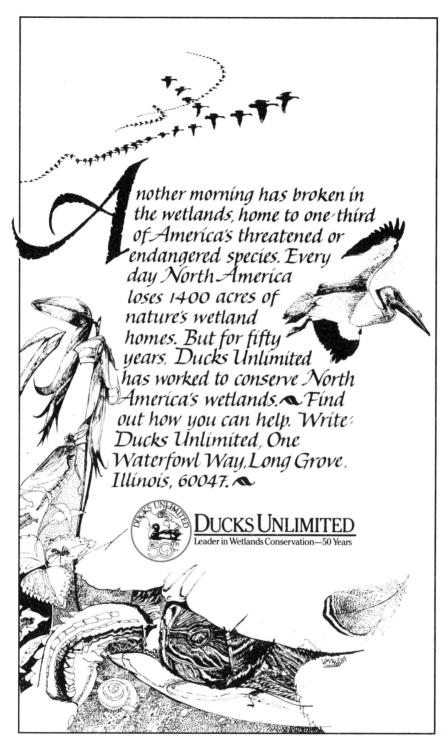

Figure 9-2

This Ducks Unlimited ad is more generalized—and can reach more potential donors: non-hunting environmentalists as well as hunters.

Yet, that's exactly what this writer does when he signs the letter:

> Sincerely,
> Jonathan F. Cunningham III

Signing the letter with a middle initial and explanation of lineage automatically cuts off any rapport the fund raising writer may have established with the reader. It's the written equivalent of donning top hat and tails. It pushes the reader off to arm's length by saying "I'm not one of you."

Better to sign this letter:

> Sincerely,
> Jonathan Cunningham
>   or
> Thank you with all my heart,
> Jon Cunningham

The true fund raising communicator takes ego off-line, because ego is an *anti*-rapport factor.

Establishing the Voice of Authority Through Public Relations

Classic public relations was founded on image.

Today, conscious attempts at pure image-building can fail on two levels—the intended target *and* the media itself. Since the word "investigative" too often precedes the title "reporter," an apparently innocent news release can generate a negative article.

Any public relations program can link your name with single unrelated events or news hooks: influential for a day or a week...but falling short in long-term image. Random publicity and "shoot-from-the-hip" reactions to news events aren't true public relations.

That's the distinction between merely serviceable public relations and *dynamic* public relations. Publicizing the hard facts about a company in a news release is less valuable than tying news releases to target-audience benefit. Relating your quasi-news to individuals exposed to the message is the difference between cold facts and a dynamic public relations program.

Tying Public Relations to Its Targets

If the purpose of a news release is to describe a product, include what the product does to improve the user's lifestyle or business. If the release describes a service, relate the service to the reader.

This results in a strategic public relations program orchestrated from your core marketing objectives. The parallel between public relations and benefit-advertising is absolute.

Marketers can cite instance after instance in which a well-placed news release accounted for considerably more business than an ad in the same publication. A well-written news release combines image and response.

Dynamic public relations programs establish you or your company as the voice of authority within the field. They combine image with a subtly introduced reader-benefit: By doing business with you the reader is dealing with the top. In the ever-changing marketplace, the public connects your name with your achievements. The effect on your marketing is profound.

A Word of Caution

Until the marriage of image and response is completely consummated, a word of caution: ''Image'' writers tend to disconnect news releases from the real world, rhapsodizing without making a marketing point.

''Response'' writers tend to spew out user-benefits without romance. A good point made brutally becomes an irritant rather than a spur.

The path between these two extremes is where effectiveness lies. A publication is more likely to print your news release and a television station is more likely to air your video if it isn't either a) apparently unrelated to readers or viewers or b) blatantly self-serving.

Dynamic public relations is more than a strategic marketing tool; it can be your strategic marketing weapon.

Use dynamic public relations to accomplish both long-term and short-term goals. Make it your business to recognize each change in the marketplace and adapt your public relations strategy to capitalize on the change rather than fall victim to it.

How Retailers Can Maintain Market Image While Ringing Up the Cash Register

According to a Deloitte and Touche retail survey, advertising as a percentage of sales is declining.

In 1988, 61 percent of retailers surveyed said they wouldn't change their ad budgets—and 13 percent said they would decrease ad spending. In 1989, 52 percent said they would not change while 21 percent said they'd decrease ad spending.

In 1990, on the verge of a recession, advertising trade publications reported dramatic declines in magazine advertising as well as anticipated cutbacks in all media by major advertisers. Retailers, led by giant chains (many of whom were and are trying to avoid toppling into a bankruptcy chapter-11 snakepit), were and are cutting budgets.

Commentators cry, "You shouldn't be cutting budgets, you should be increasing them." But where does the money come from?

Researchers and analysts predict retailers will be cutting *media* ad spending even deeper in the uncertain future.

Why? 1990s sales trends are weak. While department stores are reducing inventory, cutting down on available selections of merchandise, a good part of ad dollars formerly allocated to TV and newspapers are being diverted to experimental direct marketing programs. For example, Bloomingdale's By Mail has become a separate entity from its retailing parent.

Smart Retailing Parallels All Smart Marketing: Image + Response

Grocery stores learned two generations ago that putting a discount coupon in the paper brings store traffic.

Today, free-standing inserts in metropolitan newspapers generate redemption of billions of cents-off coupons. Consumers switch brands based on a twenty-five cent coupon. So much for brand loyalty!

Recognition of buyer-fickleness might cause the naive marketer to assume image counts for nothing. Not so. The excitement of a cents-off coupon is heightened by recognition that we're saving money not on an unknown generic product but on a heavily-advertised brand whose name and wrapper are instantly identifiable.

Retailers in non-food areas have discovered the coupon. Instead of the hackneyed headline, "10% Off Every Suit in the Store," they're seeing better results from "This Coupon Entitles You to 10% Off Every Suit in the Store."

The difference is one of primitive psychology, not fact. Drug stores may have a film-processing discount coupon sitting on the counter. The total availability couldn't be more obvious; but the magic of coupons overrides the obvious.

Retailers who advertise any type of merchandise sale without specifying a price are asking for lowered response. Some discount catalogs, in pages advertising name-brand computers and cameras say, "Call for price." I hope this is because they're forbidden to advertise the price and not because they think it's smart marketing. It isn't.

Smart marketing brings in buyers with as few steps as possible. "Call for price" is implicitly a *two-step* conversion. The prospective buyer has to make two decisions, not one—first, the decision to call; then the decision to buy.

High-fashion ads often exclude as many logical target-prospects as they include. Some are aimed at a coterie, an in-group who need no education to interpret the oblique sales message. But to the outsider who might buy, an incomprehensible message cries out silently.

Marketing Blinders Prevent Peripheral Vision

In fund raising...in public relations...in retailing...and in every facet of business and consumer marketing, partial education coupled with prejudice is the principal obstacle to effective salesmanship.

If only parading around the office, waving an ad and exclaiming, "This one is an award-winner!" were a capital offense. If only deleting any evidence of romance and imagination were reason to be drummed out of the corps.

"They won't buy it if you don't convince them they want it" is not only a proper battle-cry for the mid-1990s; it's a truism.

Marketing Checklist — Chapter 9

Fund Raising

☐ 1. Have you maintained your image while asking for dollars in your fund raising campaign?
☐ 2. Have you gathered the reader into your arms?
☐ 3. Have you massaged the reader's ego?
☐ 4. Have you tapped into the reader's guilt?
☐ 5. Have you determined the prospective donor's reason for giving?
☐ 6. Does your plea speak to the reader *personally*?
☐ 7. Is your appeal warm?
☐ 8. Does your writing take your ego off-line so rapport remains intact?

Public Relations

☐ 1. Are your news releases dynamic? Or just cold facts?

☐ 2. Are your news releases tied to reader-benefit?

☐ 3. Does your release establish you or your company as the authority in your field?

☐ 4. Do your news releases seem to be genuine news? Or are they blatantly self-serving?

☐ 5. Have you adapted your public relations strategy to changes in the marketplace and changes in *your* position within the marketplace?

Retail

☐ 1. Are you using coupons in your brand advertising?

☐ 2. Are your coupons specific in their offer (specific brands, specific prices)?

CHAPTER *10*

Pitfalls to Avoid: An Illustrated Checklist

When you're creating effective advertising, what to avoid may be just as easy to recognize as what to do.

I present to you a *partial* checklist to help improve your advertising. The questions and examples given are my opinion of good and bad advertising...no, effective and ineffective advertising. You may disagree; but temper your disagreement with positive opinions of your own, based not on personal prejudices but on solid principles of communication.

Please don't defend advertising with statements such as, "The client liked it." Please *do* defend advertising with statements such as, "We tested this against other approaches, and it pulled best."

My first opinion—and if you regard this as iconoclastic, you and/or your clients have to be in peril:

> The way to gauge the effectiveness of advertising is its pulling power within the specific target group at whom it's aimed, NOT intramural backslapping, awards which ignore results, or how pretty the ad looks in your portfolio or the commercial looks on your reel.

Effectiveness is the yardstick, the criterion, the litmus test. I defend this on two grounds:

1. It's an advertising truism.
2. Any other gauge is unrelated to the end-purpose of advertising—marketing

With this prelude, here are a few of the questions I suggest you ask yourself before setting type or turning on studio lights.

1. Do Your Headlines and Subheads Involve the Reader?

We already have agreed that a headline's function is to grab attention *on a beneficial level* and pull the reader into the subhead or text. (The purpose of a subhead is to induce the reader to read the rest of the ad.)

The best way to accomplish these goals with your headlines and subheads is to recognize your readers' interests and aim your headlines and subheads squarely at those interests.

Here's an easy tip for your "swipe" file. Take a look at the headlines and subheads you see on the covers of magazines displayed at the newsstand. One on the cover of a business magazine:

> Head: "How Am I Doing?" what Your Boss Can't
> Tell You
> Subhead: To get the scoop on your future, do your own
> performance checkup.

A travel magazine:

> Head: More Sun for the Money
> Subhead: How to escape winter without fiscal pain

A cooking magazine:

> Head: Entertaining from a small kitchen
> Subhead: Tips, tactics, and tempting food

Comparing magazine cover headlines to advertising headlines isn't quite fair because people generally buy magazines to read the *articles*—not the advertising. But a powerful parallel should have grabbed you. These headlines promise a *benefit* to the reader. What those headlines say—the way they're written, calculated to tease you into the inner pages—is the reason people pick up, say, *Newsweek* over *Time*. . .or *People* over *US* at the newsstand.

Even if the subject matter of the articles is the same—the cover headlines are usually the determining factor. They are, in effect, the headlines advertising the magazines. We should choose the same weapons in our rhetorical advertising arsenal.

Differing Uses of the Same Weapons

The difference? Within the pages of that same magazine, we're competing for the reader's attention, not only with the articles but with our competitors' advertising. We have to snatch the reader's attention away from the magazine article—and we have to do a better job of it than our competition does.

How do we do it? Suppose you wear glasses. You're reading the newspaper one morning and you notice your arms aren't long enough to hold the newspaper far enough away to read the small print. Uh-oh. Time for bifocals. Translation: You're approaching middle age. Has anyone noticed how old you are yet? If you start wearing bifocals, *everyone* will know. No way are you going to wear bifocals!

If you're a bifocal manufacturer, how does your advertising generate interest in a product nobody wants to buy?

Figure 10-1 shows how one lens manufacturer does it. The photograph shows a forty-something-year-old man wearing glasses. The headline reads:

> The First Thing You'll Notice When You Wear Our Bifocals is that Nobody Notices.

Would that get your attention? You bet it would. . .IF you're a logical target. Would you read the body copy? Of course. . .IF you're a logical target. And what do you find in the body copy? A toll-free phone number directing you to eyewear specialists who carry this brand of bifocal lenses. Will you call? I'll bet you will. . .IF you're a logical target.

The inevitable key to effectiveness: Appealing to logical targets. The inevitable key to failure: Appealing to others in your office.

Figure 10-1

Logical targets for this product will be drawn into the copy after reading this benefit-oriented headline.

What Are They Selling? And to Whom?

Let's look at another ad (figure 10-2). This is a double-page spread. The headline:

> There's a Word for Business People Who Don't Use Sky-
> tel. Lunch.

The photo shows two men sitting together with huge indistinct shadows looming over their heads. When we scrutinize the shadows we can just make out one is the shadow of a lamb (I think) and one is the shadow of a wolf. Oh. One man is "lunch" to the other?

See the mismatch? The headline skews its meaning, because "Lunch" suggests more leisure time—a *positive* result. Had the headline read

> There's an Expression for Business People Who Don't
> Use Skytel. Lunch for Those Who Do.

we'd have understood immediately what this writer wants us to think, instead of floundering and then *revising* our original reaction.

A revised reaction is never as strong as an original, reinforced reaction.

The body copy of the Skytel ad:

> In the eat or be eaten world of business, there is no re-
> ward for coming in second. To win a sale, a case, a client,
> you have to get there first. This means it's not just what
> you know, but when you know it that counts.
>
> Which explains why those who would rather be preda-
> tor than prey depend on Skytel. As the industry leader,
> our list of subscribers reads like a Who's Who of Fortune
> 500 companies, national sales and service...

And on it goes. We don't know what exactly this advertiser is selling until the very bottom of the column. And a busy executive probably won't read that far because in an "eat or be eaten world," if an executive takes the time to try to decipher this ad, that individual most assuredly would "come in second" with no reward...lunch for the person who spent time more profitably.

167

Figure 10-2

This ad suffers from message ''slippage.'' The message is clever but indirect, and the reader has to work to understand the intended message.

169

Clever but Indirect: Message Slippage

That's a wry comment, of course; but what happened here? The creative team producing this ad worked hard to come up with an original, never-before-used idea. And somewhere along the way, they lost sight of *who* would be reading the ad...and slipped into "clever and indirect."

Indirect messages suffer from "slippage"...reactions oblique to the intended reaction. Generating oblique reactions works only if you're deliberately obfuscating, which no effective advertising message does.

More's the pity—because judging from the coupon in the ad, they wanted *someone* to respond (even though the coupon doesn't tell us what we're responding to). Will a salesperson call us? Or will we receive a brochure with more information and prices? or can we order this product direct by dialing the phone number?).

The Non-Involving Headline

Another ad's headline (figure 10-3):

The power of Productivity.

This headline isn't reader-involving. But because the ad is a huge full newspaper page, its very size catches the reader's attention.
Maybe the subhead will involve the reader.

If you think diverting two rivers to clean stables is hard
work, try managing a modern corporation.

I see the coupon, so the ad is a response ad. But WHAT ARE THEY SELLING? The body copy doesn't shed any light on the question; but aside from that, both headline and subhead are too obscure to lead the reader anywhere.
If your question is, "Then how would *you* write this ad?" I could give you a flip answer, the way Hercules, the hero of this ad, would have answered: "I was hired to clean the stables, not refill them."

Figure 10-3

If anyone reads this ad, the logical question is: ''What are they trying to sell?''

 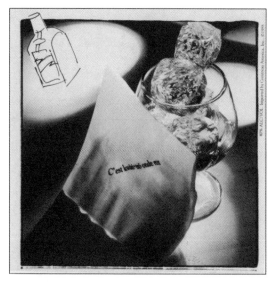

Figure 10-4 and 10-5

To the reader unfamiliar with this product, the advertiser is saying, "We know something you don't know."

Not being Herculean, I'll ask you: Can you see the problems in this ad? Of course you can. All the headline does is *announce*. But announce *what*? What does the announcement mean to the reader? All the subhead does is explain what the illustration is—but what does it mean to the reader?

If "diverting two rivers" is an analogy to diverting the energies of two corporate departments, write the headline so it involves the reader— within his field of interest—and induces him to respond.

Rewrite the ad? Who would *dare*—not knowing what the ad is about?

"Insider" Jargon: A 1990s Way to Infuriate the Reader

What's worse than writing an obscure headline? Writing an obscure headline using inside jargon.

Figures 10-4 and 10-5 ran on consecutive pages. The headlines are the same:

C'est kwan-tro onde rox

What are these ads selling?

Before you decide I'm hurling stones from the safety of my ivory tower office, let me assure you I ask an assortment of people what they think of an ad before I hit. I showed these ads around. Some of the reactions I got were:

"I haven't the slightest idea of what they're selling."

"It's liquor of some sort, right? Why don't they show the bottle?"

"What are these dirty napkins?"

"Sest kwan tro ondee rox? What does it mean? If this is one of those creative department tricks, you'd better translate it for me."

Someone familiar with the product already might know it's a French liqueur, just from phoneticizing the "headline": C'est Cointreau-on-the-rocks." But what about those people who don't speak French? Are they going to sound it out so they say, "Sest Cointreau on de rocks?" And then are they going to buy the product just because they got the joke?

> When the reader thinks you're saying, "I know something you don't," that reader will be annoyed or infuriated. Don't let a mad desire to be clever lead you into non-communicating camouflage.
>
> The more you obscure your message, the more you *exclude* those who aren't already pre-sold on what you're marketing.

---

2. Does Your Illustration Work With or Against Your Headline?

We've agreed to involve our readers in our headlines; now, are we extending them the same involvement with the visuals?

To do this effectively, we need three "yes" answers to key questions: 1) Have the writer and art director agreed on the ad? 2) Has the writer seen the visuals? 3) Has the art director read the copy? Sometimes we wonder whether these two people have even been introduced to each other.

Unnecessary Visual Mismatches

Take a look at figure 10-6. The headline reads:

> Holidays are made happier simply by shopping at Sherman Oaks Galleria.

173

The two women pictured don't look happy at all. They look dyspeptic . . . or ready to shoot someone. (Maybe the writer meant these two would be happier *then they are now* if they'd only taxi over to Sherman Oaks Galleria? Please, ladies, I'll even pay the fare!)

"Holidays are made happier simply by shopping at Sherman Oaks Galleria."

Figure 10-6

The message in the visual doesn't match the written message.

174

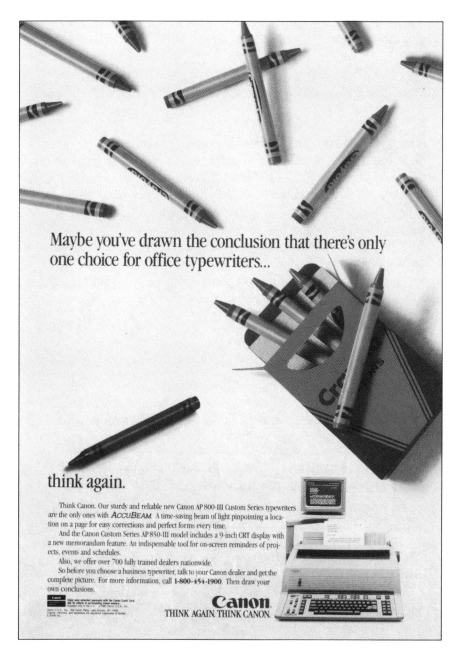

Figure 10-7

The gap between the ad's visual and the product is too wide: It's an incomprehensible visual puzzle and the reader won't understand the analogy.

175

Figure 10-7 makes us wonder which came first—headline or photo? The headline:

> Maybe you've drawn the conclusion that there's only one
> choice for office typewriters...
> think again.

The photo shows a box of blue Crayolas. A red crayola sits alone.

The reader asks, if puzzles are appealing, What do crayons have to do with typewriters? Do we get to choose between the colors red and blue in typewriter ribbons? A choice of colors in the typewriter itself? Or are they telling us a typewriter is easier to use than a Crayola? What's the connection between copy and art?

The average reader probably won't even get far enough to ask those questions—because the analogy between typewriters and crayons is *so* far away from normal comparative comprehension it's not even engaging... even if you're in the market for a new typewriter. The response number is listed " for more information." How many calls do you imagine they received from this ad?

Visual puzzles in which elements have no apparent connection *after* the reader has studied the elements are confounding rather than engrossing.

Reserve such techniques for puzzle books and meetings of the Mensa Society. By leaving the typical reader out of the loop, they fail as involvement techniques.

What Are We Looking At?—No Message Transmitted

The headline in Figure 10-8 says:

> Our commitment to quality goes back a long way. And
> ahead even further.

We'd expect the photo to relate to that headline, but we don't know what it is we're looking at. A museum? Is Alexander Graham Bell's first phone somewhere in that museum? It might be...but we can't see it. The book entitled *Economic Control of Manufactured Product* by W.A. Shewart is shown on the far right. Maybe that's what's in this museum. But the art direction is so disjointed, we're not inclined to read this ad. So

Our commitment to quality goes back a long way. And ahead even further.

It started with the genius of Alexander Graham Bell. And from the beginning, AT&T has been committed to helping the people of the world communicate better.

To fulfill this commitment, AT&T has always placed quality at the heart of everything we do.

To us, quality is what our customers say it is. So every product and service we provide has to live up to what they expect.

Tomorrow, this dedication will enable us to provide this same quality to the people of the world in new ways.

Funny, how the future seems to repeat itself.

The 1920s Quality Control

Walter A. Shewhart of AT&T Bell Laboratories pioneered in quality control during the 1920s. His book, *Economic Control of Quality of Manufactured Product*, provided a foundation for the science of statistical quality control and has become an industry standard.

Today The AT&T Worldwide Intelligent Network

Today's AT&T network is the most advanced telecommunications network in the world. The quality of your call is checked even before you start speaking. In effect, today's AT&T network actually performs 75 million service checks per day. That's how many calls we complete.

Tomorrow Global Telecommunity

In the future, we envision a world where people can communicate information in any form as easily as making a phone call today–even gathering information from the libraries of the world at the touch of a button.

AT&T
The right choice.

Figure 10-8

The average reader won't know what kind of "quality" this advertiser is talking about since the art direction is out of sync with the message.

When it comes to undiscovered destinations, Maggie is one step ahead.

Figure 10-9

Will the average reader recognize this ad as any kind of message?

the average reader will probably never know what kind of "quality" this advertiser is talking about.

The ad is purely an "image" ad. But the image is murky—and the message will probably go unnoticed. What a waste.

Figure 10-9 ran in a men's fashion magazine. It shows a woman racing across the page. The tiny reversed-out headline reads:

> When it comes to undiscovered destinations, Maggie is
> one step ahead.

Huh? The reader might look at the next page to see if that's where the ad continues (which it doesn't), but more likely, he'll flip past it without

When Maggie does the test driving...magazine readers flock to the showroom.

TURBO

Magazines make things happen.

Figure 10-10

Another pretty picture, but we still don't find much of a message...

even noticing. And why should he? It's just a photo. The ad has no message.

Figure 10-10 shows an ad which ran in another issue of that same men's magazine. Again, it shows "Maggie"—in an unidentifiable car this time. The headline reads:

> When Maggie does the test driving...magazine readers
> flock to the showroom.
> Magazines make things happen.

Ah, now we're beginning to understand what they're selling here: magazine advertising. But in a men's magazine? Well, maybe media buyers read this magazine, too. We still don't quite have a message here. But we sure do have a pretty picture.

Figure 10-11 shows another version of the ad in figure 10-10, inserted in an advertising trade magazine. This one puts persuasive copy to work. The headline and subhead:

> How to sell $103 billion worth of new cars.
> Put Maggie to work.

This ad does give us a message to read.

> A magazine ad gives your best prospects the chance to "hold your car in their hands." They get more information—a better look at features...which probably explains why auto marketers took a hard look at their ad spending last year.

One can only assume whoever originated and inserted these ads finally took a hard look at their own spending—and decided a pretty picture wasn't enough to convey a strong selling message.

Advertising messages are seldom the primary reason our prospects pick up a magazine, or turn on the television or radio. We're interlopers. Those people don't care what we think we're saying to them. In fact, our message is generally something they try to ignore.

Our first job is to overcome indifference to our message. Our second job is to make it impossible for readers, viewers, or listeners to resist buying our product.

Our total job is to look at every ad through the eyes of the person at whom the message is aimed.

Figure 10-11

Here, finally, a persuasive message aimed at a logical target: Advertising media buyers.

Figure 10-12

An appealing ad, but the main copy never mentions the product or the need for the product.

3. Are You Attacking the Assumption of Reader Indifference?

We can assume readers are indifferent as they chance upon our messages. They may be antagonistic, apathetic, or if we're unusually lucky, enthusiastic; but usually they're indifferent.

Transforming neutrality into enthusiasm is mandatory for the professional communicator. Let's see how some professionals—and by that I mean people who get paid to do this—have fulfilled this task.

Take a look at figure 10-12. This ad for a luggage company was placed in a travel magazine. The visual is appealing to a traveler. Pleasantly framed and laid out, it shows an interesting European building and inviting place to enjoy strudel and watch the world go by. The copy is written in first person editorial style. It's an easy read—and the story the writer relates about his trip to Germany will probably interest the reader of this magazine . . . who will read it and then move onto the next travel article. The problem: This reader probably won't be influenced to buy this brand of luggage.

Why? Because neither luggage nor need for luggage is ever mentioned in the many words of copy, except offhandedly in the tagline, ''Go there on a Lark!''

The only words about the product are squished underneath the main copy block. Set in seven-point italics, it's almost impossible to read—and the reader has no reason to read it because the main copy block builds no sales arguments and initiates no benefits for owning this particular brand of luggage. Or any luggage at all, for that matter. The ad hasn't overcome the reader's indifference.

Compare this ad with figures 10-13 and 10-14, much smaller ads which ran on consecutive pages of another travel magazine.

The headline in figure 10-13:

The 3-In-One Garment Bag by Andiamo

In this quarter-page ad, the visual easily manages to show what the entire bag looks like, inside and out. Better still, it turns all the bag's features into benefits by showing us just exactly what we can do with this bag. If we want more details, those details are there for us. Even though the type is almost as tiny as the type at the bottom of figure 10-12, this typeface is easy to read.

A second, parallel ad by this advertiser appears on the facing page.

Andiamo has deeper pockets than ever.

The visual shows a $100 bill in a pocket of the bag. To clarify the message and tie it to the ad on the facing page, a reverse at the bottom reads:

Save $100 with the 3-In-One Garment Bag

Included in the body copy is a toll-free phone number to find a participating retailer.

Now *that's* how to overcome the reader's indifference!

Figure 10-13

The copy and the visuals show the benefits of using this product.

Figure 10-14

The second ad on a facing page gives the reader an incentive to buy this brand.

Overcoming reader indifference is no more complicated than grabbing your reader's attention, using benefits to sell, giving an incentive (greed being such a primary motivator, incentives invariably go a long way toward overcoming indifference), and making sure your prospect knows where to find you.

Telling the Reader What to Do

Figure 10-15 is an ad for computer software designed for writers. The software proofreads written documents for grammatical and usage errors. The headline reads:

>   Read It And Reap.

"Read It" *does* tell the reader what to do. "Reap"? Well...we'll excuse this failed attempt at clever wordplay because except for the headline the ad is literally perfect.

The document pictured is the "involvement device"—it's a contest. The memo addressed to "anyone interested in writing improvement" from "Ken Dickens, ad writer." (I've got to hand it to this guy. He's one of the few copywriters who has ever found a legitimate way to sign his work.)

The purpose of the contest is for the reader to find the nineteen grammatical and usage problems in the typed memo. Find them all, and they'll send you the product, free. Can't find them all? Don't worry. They'll send you a demo disk just for trying. What writer can resist?

This ad is a wonderfully inventive way to involve your reader, distribute free samples to your market group, collect names for your database, and get a conscientious writer interested in your product (*unconscientious* writers won't care—and they're not your target-group anyway).

The Benefit of Timing

Figure 10-16 shows a bound-in magazine insert. The headline reads:

>   Gold.
>   Rush.

and shows a picture of the product, an AT&T gold credit card.

In 1990 AT&T unleashed a hurricane of integrated advertising for this product: Full page newspaper ads. Television ads. Direct mail. Telemarketing. Their predominant message: If you become a 1990 member, you get the card free for life.

Wow! To anyone who carries a credit card, that's a great offer! Most credit cards will give charter members free membership for only a year or six months. After that, the fee is anywhere from $24 to $75 for a gold card. So AT&T's gold card offer minced the competition's. AT&T made it easy to apply by phone (understandably, since they're a phone company) ...and many did.

Then again, many others never got around to responding to the first promotional blast. After all, the average citizen is bombarded with credit card offers every day.

So what makes this little insert special? Not just the offer, but the *timing* of the offer.

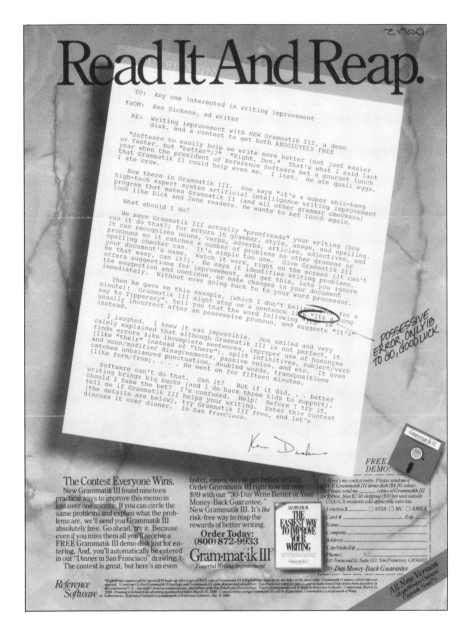

Figure 10-15

Despite the weak wordplay in the headline, this ad effectively involves the reader by rewarding him or her to literally scribble all over it.

This insert was bound into the December 1990 issue of a magazine.

The offer was the same—free lifetime membership—but only if the reader became a *1990* charter member.

A limited-time offer can be just what an advertiser needs to overcome reader indifference. Because the phone number was displayed so prominently—and a phone call is so easy to make—you just know this advertiser received a lot of December calls.

4. Does Your Ad Tell the Truth?

Sometimes advertisers, in their zeal to overcome a prospect's indifference, concoct an exciting offer too good to deliver.

Their reasoning, I suppose, is if they get the customer into the store they'll make the sale anyway, no matter what they promised.

Figure 10-16

The timing of an offer can effectively overcome the reader's indifference and prompt an immediate response.

Problem: Once your prospect decides you're stretching the truth too far, he will never, ever grant you an audience again—no matter how good your product or how legitimate your offer may be afterwards.

The $200 Misunderstanding

Art Linkletter was chosen as commercial spokesperson for a brand of easy chairs targeted to seniors. Hard to find a more credible spokesperson if you want to advertise to that age group.

The advertiser put together a commercial to get customers into the stores where their chair is sold. How to overcome consumer indifference?

Call for a "Free trade-In Certificate" worth $200. The offer: "Trade in any old chair in your home and get $200 toward the purchase of the Classic Model Contour Chair of your choice."

That's a good offer for anyone interested in this product. Two hundred dollars is a sizeable discount and likely to lure prospects into the store.

Let's say you called the toll-free response number and received your $200 Trade-In Certificate. You hauled an old kitchen chair out of the cellar and, chair and certificate in hand, you marched off to buy your new Contour Chair.

You leave your chair in the car when you get to the store because you feel silly lugging it around while you look at the assortment of chairs. Besides, it's too heavy and you want to browse unencumbered.

You choose your chair, find out how much it costs, and decide it's right for you. You collect your chair and your $200 Trade-In Certificate from the car and confidently walk back into the store.

Suppose the retailer promptly tells you the price he gave you five minutes before was the wrong price. He's going to have to charge you more. How is this possible?

It's possible because, when you watched the commercial, you probably didn't notice the tiny print at the bottom of the television screen. It said, "Trade-in promotion may increase price of chair."

Now, promising you a $200 trade-in towards the price of your new chair, and then not giving it to you because of an unnoticed disclaimer, isn't an advertising lie. But, at best, it's a nodding acquaintance with the truth.

The retailer may make the sale in spite of the ruse, but he's not going to make any points for future sales. And word-of-mouth may do more damage than a few sales could possibly be worth.

5. Are You Emphasizing Your Customers, Not Yourself?

How many times have you given in to chest-thumping in your ads? Sure, you're a terrific company, and you want everyone to know it. But

Figure 10-17

Chest-thumping isn't any way to introduce yourself to a prospect—and you'll never get close enough to make a sale.

telling 'em who you are and what you do without relating it to your prospects leaves them saying, "Yeah, but what's in it for *me?*"

The Wrong Way to Say Hello to a Prospective Customer

Figure 10-17 is an ad for a financial group. (Does the typical reader have any idea what a "financial group" is?)

> Whatever your financial needs,
> our numbers give you an edge.

The first words in the headline are the tip-off: "Whatever your financial needs." Sure, they say "your" in the headline—isn't that relating it to the prospect?

Nope.

"Whatever your financial needs" says, in effect, to the reader, "We don't know who you are, we don't know what you want—and we don't *care.*"

Now is that any way to say hello to a new customer?

Then the reader is regaled with a list of numbers as proof that this company is "one of America's strongest financial services organizations" to give "individuals and businesses an advantage" (an advantage for what?) and has earned "Moody's top rating" (Aaa).

Does the reader have a clue what they're talking about?

Copy goes on to say "customers now number seven and a half million, and growing." That *is* a heck of a lot of people. Puzzling though that they service 7,500,000 people: yet, by running an *introductory* chest-thumping ad, they obviously assume (correctly) the readers of this publication don't know who they are.

Then, at the bottom of the copy block, they tell me; "We want you to feel like you're our only customer." Oh, thank you. After you've emphasized those 7½ million others, now I feel special.

Oh, yes an advertiser has plenty of ways of pointing out both a) size/stability and b) personalized attention. Self-glorification *isn't* one of those ways; a message from the president, or some testimonials, are.

This advertiser does give me a phone number to call to "learn more" about "The Principal Edge." But what are the chances I'll call? Pretty slim, because the ad hasn't given me, the reader, anything to grab onto. All I have are generalities and numbers that don't mean anything to me as a prospect.

Figure 10-18

Copy focused on "we" is rarely as persuasive as copy focused on "you."

The Perils of "Needs" as a Noun

Will another financial company make me feel better? I turn to a double-page spread showing a cloud bank with a building peeking out of it (figure 10-18). The headline:

> We can help make your financial outlook a little clearer.

I certainly hope so after the last ad I read. And does this company zero in on what *I* might need from them? No again.

> We offer innovative insurance and investment products
> designed to meet a variety of financial needs.

"Needs" as a noun is far too weak to cause a reader to lift phone or pen. These two financial services ads hammer the point home.

This advertiser hopes the company has enough "products" (another turn-off word) to cover my financial "needs" somewhere. Copy continues:

> When you deal with us, you're dealing with an organiza-
> tion that serves more than one million policyholders...

Well, okay, they're big too. But the ad has *zero* reader personalization, despite its expensive two-page, four color bleed production. So much for feeling selected from the crowd here.

Their tagline:

> The power of the pyramid is working for you.

(Allow me to be picky here—I know this refers to the company's building, but "pyramid power" really is out of fashion.)

It Isn't All That Difficult

Attacking non-communicating ads is easy, especially for people in the advertising business. We all do it because we all love it. It makes us super-equal with those giant companies whose committee-generated ads are so far off-target.

Then what?

Wryness notwithstanding, when an onlooker, critic, or antagonist asks, "Then what would you have done?" I hope your answer is the same as mine. "I'd have arrowed that ad at a specific target, telling a specific group of people exactly what I want them to do."

This isn't all that difficult, if you can think like those ad readers outside your office.

Headline Pitfalls to Avoid

1. Steer clear of headlines and subheads which fail to involve your reader.
2. Never assume your reader knows as much as you do.
3. Stifle the urge to be subtle or obscure.

Visual Pitfalls to Avoid

1. Veto visuals which don't reinforce the written message, creating confusion.
2. Replace or eliminate visuals which create confusion by overpowering the message.
3. Don't fight to include "clever" visuals as substitutes for a genuine message.

Motivational Pitfalls to Avoid

1. Don't become so enamored of your product you forget that others won't know how good it is unless you show them.
2. Don't assume, even if you *show* how good your product is, people will rush out to buy it. Sometimes they need an extra nudge...and incentive, an expiration date, or promise of exclusivity.

Offer Pitfalls to Avoid

1. Fine print, tiny type you hope the reader won't see, or asterisks in your print advertising, and mini-supers in your television advertising aren't reinforcements of claimed integrity. Instead, they tend to put your customers on guard.
2. Offers with strings or hidden disclaimers will probably do more damage to your image and future sales than the initial traffic they bring in.

Ego Pitfalls to Avoid

1. Never assume the reader cares about you. The reader cares only about what you can do for him or her.
2. Don't use nondescript words such as "needs" or "product" to describe what you have or do. These draw no image for the reader.
3. When combining claims of size and power with the promise of personalized attention, word your message so the reader feels special, not one of a mob.

CHAPTER *11*

After 2001, What? An Iconoclastic Look to the Future

By the year 2000 a "full service" agency will be an agency which straddles every aspect of communications.

Integration *will* happen. In fact, it's already happening because integration is the next logical move in marketing. Will the union be smooth, or two unlike pieces crazy-glued together? The answer depends on whether proponents of the two disciplines are enthusiastic or reluctant.

Some of the very biggest advertising agencies—Leo Burnett, for example—have announced total integration of their conventional and direct marketing departments.

These "hybrid" agencies have come to realize the best way to help their clients grow (and, incidentally, help the agencies grow along with them) is to cultivate, nurture and expand, and include in the strategy meeting "other" agency departments. ("Other" agency departments: anything other than general media advertising units, including the direct marketing, promotional, event marketing, and retail departments of the agency.)

"Get Off My Turf"

The war is over, even if all the peace treaties haven't yet been signed. Integration is too well-established and too logical for traditionalists to discount it.

Still, we seem to have pockets of intramural warfare, like rival street-gangs or wolves claiming territory without reason other than "This is mine."

As the voices of all internal marketing departments become stronger and are included into each client's overall marketing strategy, keep in mind: When each department remains a separate profit center within the agency, prepare for a turf war.

Here's why: No matter how lofty your aim to make all talents and disciplines available to each client's marketing plan, if each department remains separate—as a separate profit center—the goals of each department head will naturally reflect that department's unintegrated battle plan. A department head's major concern will be protecting or enlarging his department's share of the profit pie (possibly at the expense of the client's marketing effectiveness).

Separate profit centers automatically reward separate department heads, *not* for contributing to the client's profits but for the profits their departments bring in. In the mid-1990s, this tunnelvision causes critics to call advertising agencies the names they deserve if they don't amend this obsolete and selfish attitude.

Conversely, mixing the profits of all departments into the same pot dictates a statesmanlike change. The client's integrated marketing plan becomes the primary goal, and separate department profits become—as they should—secondary.

Taking ego and jealous departments off the line enables agencies to present a comprehensive battle plan to clients, unhampered by tradition and responsibility boundaries.

What a good move!

Client-pressures are increasing—for better use of dollars, faster response to competitors' moves, and a total understanding of the marketing mix. Every issue of every trade paper testifies to this. So an agency's positive integration, reducing internal competition, helps improve not just agency stability but marketing effectiveness.

Who's Gonna Teach It?

Schools of journalism and departments of advertising and mass communications now have courses in most of the major communications disciplines. Yet too many instructors, alumni of a different era, still preach sovereignty.

What happens? Unwitting students pick up a mindless prejudice and carry it off with them to the workplace.

> Education without battlefield practice has its own problem of obsolescence which increases exponentially every semester... and generates this same problem for the students who absorb an obsolete doctrine. The more vertical an education, the more arrogantly defensive the competitive position. Despite their own vertical education, instructors should take a statesmanlike view toward marketing disciplines other than or more recent than their own.

And what about battlefield-practiced training? Back in the mid-1970s when advertising agencies decided training programs were an unaffordable "extra," many eliminated training programs from their budgets, relying instead on skimming the cream off the current crop of advertising school graduates. Yet today, agency scouts, seeing a glimmer of raw talent in the student pool, scoop up these talented students even before they graduate (and before a rival agency scoops them first).

Who, then, in this era of sliced budgets, will supervise a student's education after the student has joined the agency?

Formal in-agency training still seems to be a page from the past. Too many young turks talented (or cunning) enough to survive the initial shake-out period have learned their own nasty two-part Successful Advertising catechism:

1. If it's an award-winner, it must be good advertising.
2. If it's an award-winner, *I* must be good.

That attitude has led to a whole generation of advertising people who use only one yardstick to measure their ad: How will it stack up in the eyes of the Clio judges? (Just in case you haven't heard of it: A "Clio" is an advertising award lionized by art directors and copywriters.)

Few battle-scarred agency pros have or will take the time to formally train the juniors. So recruits take sustenance wherever they can get it.

Too often lack of training results in a junior creative person following an ultimately miserable path: admiring, then emulating one small campaign component—an ad that made it into the awards book. Strategy, positioning, and where that ad fits into the building blocks of the total campaign, are often ignored unless these elements are taught.

That's where many conventional agencies with their pre-1990s corporate philosophy fail the young creative talent. The disciplines of direct marketing and promotion are too seldom taught, or even considered part of, a whole and integrated strategy.

As a natural result, too many young students of advertising begin to believe these disciplines are beneath them. And that's a pity because direct marketing, with its absolute and unassailable method of keeping score, is actually a very good way to learn how and when marketing principles work.

The window of opportunity for advertising agencies of the future is revival of in-agency creative training of *all* marketing disciplines.

> In the 1990s, advertising agencies who want to keep their clients have to do a lot more than simply create ads. They have to offer strategic ideas NOT for winning awards BUT for marketing their clients' products.

If an advertising agency is to survive the brutally competitive 1990s, it has to grow a new generation of creative pros, experienced in every facet of marketing. The window of opportunity will slam shut in the faces of agencies who don't make a positive move to train their recruits in the logical *disciplines* of marketing.

They deserve the "Ouch!"

Future Trends

Let's face reality. No, let's grab onto reality.

Those advertising professionals who will survive the cyclical shake-out resulting from belt-tightening will be the ones who embrace not only the integration of image and direct response advertising, but also the integration of new technologies into advertising as a whole.

Those advertising professionals who will be able to identify changes in the marketplace *and* adapt their marketing strategies to those changes (while folding technological breakthroughs into the mix) will be the ones sought after as this decade deepens.

Electronic Publishing Comes into Its Own

We don't need a crystal ball to tell us electronic publishing—touted by its often-fanatical champions for the past ten years as the successor to paper communications—finally will become an advertising media contender.

Two obvious reasons for my opinion:
1. The upsurge of environmental-concern groups; and
2. The growing computer-literate marketplace.

First, consider the environmental impact on marketing. We've witnessed the world's increasing outrage over the problem of disposing solid waste materials. We're watching high-profile pressure groups who militate for reduction of irrelevant paper advertising (i.e., unsolicited advertising mail and faxes) quickly gain ground.

This isn't bad. In fact, the movement will force all of us who do use paper to rethink our marketing plans to better target our sales messages (see chapter 4). The movement most certainly will help ensure our messages are relevant to the people who receive our advertising.

Those same groups are pressuring producers of paper advertising to print on recycled/recyclable paper. Of course, recycled paper costs more ...and when costs go up, we marketers start to look for alternatives. While the price of paper rises every year, the price of the new electronic media continues to drop.

The second reason electronic publishing will come into its own is the increasing acceptance of computers.

As readers of this book already know, 40 to 50 million computers with the potential of receiving (and sending) messages to other computers sit on home and office desks in the United States alone. Kids, computer-literate from Grade 1 (where they learned to type practically before they learned to write), graduate and enter the "buyer's marketplace" every day.

Realizing the tremendous sales potential of computers requires one simple gadget—a "Modem." As of this writing more than 15 million personal computers already have them. Every one of these computers is "open" *right now* for electronic message-transfers. And none of those messages involves or requires even one sheet of paper.

Electronic publishing, while no longer unusual, enjoys a growing potential unrivalled by more traditional advertising media.

An Electronic Publishing Sampler

Demo Disks

Computer disks containing information are sent to computer owner/users. "Demo disks" have become highly sophisticated in recent years, using color, animation, sound, and even music. You can use a demo disk for lead generation, sales, tutorials, displays, catalogs, corporate communications programs—you name it. And through the use of menus, prospects can choose the features they want to see.

Ford Motor Company has successfully used demo disks for years. "Have You Driven a Ford Lately?"

takes on a whole new meaning with the demo disk they send out to prospective buyers. Their demo-disk advertising features computer "test drives" of new model cars, letting prospective buyers "experience" the road at their desktops. Ford advertises and sells these disks through direct mail and direct response ads in computer magazines, continuously updating disks as new car models are introduced. (Updating is *mandatory* in promotional demo disks.)

Have you flipped through a magazine on your computer screen yet? Many monthly "magazines" are now available on diskettes instead of paper. And here's a twist on the bound-in magazine card: Some advertisers bind demo disks into traditional paper magazines adjacent to their full-page ads.

Many catalogs are now published electronically. Computer software companies have found them especially useful for demonstrating a new piece of software. And while revising prices and reprinting a paper catalog can be an expensive proposition, revising prices in a computer-disk catalog costs less, takes less time because it doesn't have to go to the printer, and can be changed daily or even hourly.

Online Videotext

If you have a personal computer and a modem, no doubt you've dialed up an incredible assortment of information at all hours of the day and night. And you've probably enjoyed the convenience (instant shopping!) and total control (instant information!) you experienced when you tapped "online."

If you haven't, not to worry. An ever-increasing number of your customers have.

Online videotext users through subscription services such as "Prodigy on-line videotext" (developed jointly by Sears and IBM) take advantage of access to electronic banking services, stock quotes, investment advice, and financial planning. They also order goods electronically, from "on-screen" catalogs and ads.

Prodigy even became a prime means of communication between U.S. troops and their families during the Persian Gulf crisis.

As online videotext services penetrate homes and offices with computers—and as computer use increases—advertising messages on computer screens are becoming as commonplace as advertising messages on the television screens. Videotext ads can have sound, music, and visual motion, just as television does. Or an ad can be text and static graphics, paralleling magazines and newspapers.

But the difference which can change the way all advertising is presented as well as the way merchandise and services are bought in the twenty-first century is this: Videotext is *interactive*. The videotext consumer is able to "shop" at leisure by calling up specific information on his own schedule and then having both the option and the ability to place an order (and be billed for that order) immediately after making the buying decision.

And since videotext also can be used for customer surveys, you know from the data you collect exactly who subscribes to the videotext service. The potential for targeting your message to the right people is virtually limitless. Your videotext ad can be seen by the entire customer base, or you can specifically target one particular group. Computer-screen product demonstrations and sales messages can be tailored to the specific interests of a specific prospect.

Database Marketing

Personal computers are becoming so sophisticated they can bypass or replace mainframe computers in the office. One projection of development trends shows PCs will have the calculation-speeds of mainframes within this decade.

This means every marketer should be able to build, maintain, and benefit from a *database*.

So we introduce a new breed of database marketer: The specialist who can build small, niche-oriented databases on demand—and deliver the custom database to the marketer/user in PC format...or the small businessperson who buys his own database software such as Lotus Marketplace: Households.

(Lotus Marketplace *isn't* on the market because of the public outcry attending its 1991 announcement: Critics outside the ad world objected to "invasion of privacy," so Lotus withdrew the software. Inclusion here is still in order, because today's outrage is tomorrow's ho-hum.)

This software contains American household demographic information on eleven compact disks. The user can pull up age, income, and location information covering 80 million households throughout the U.S. and send mailings as targeted as major marketers.

The user then can manipulate the database on his computer at home or in the office. This means the value of data shifts from *quantity* of information to *quality* of information.

A major change resulting from this new capability: When Lotus Marketplace, and other software programs like it, finally achieve acceptance, some mailing lists will be sold (not rented as they have been for generations) and kept to be re-used.

Retail Electronic Marketing

Collecting supermarket checkout data has become a hot new marketing tool. At this writing, some test systems are plagued with problems but still show great promise.

Citicorp is testing several POS (Point of Sale) Systems, including electronic couponing and frequent shopper incentive programs. Shoppers at a particular grocery store are given a special card which is scanned at the register before the sale is rung up. The card identifies the shopper and tracks the shopper's purchases along with the shopper's name and address.

This allows packaged goods companies to deliver a variety of household-targeted programs designed to encourage loyalty, convert new prospects, and recover straying shoppers. Coupons—both electronic at checkout, or shopper-coded by mail—are issued along with incentives, rebates, and frequent-shopper programs.

Magazines, in addition to tracking their in-store sales on a daily basis, can check their subscriber lists against the database to determine whether their readers buy the types of products advertised—creating buyer profiles for their advertisers and strengthening their argument for additional space sales.

Since shopping habits of individual customer names can be tracked easily, this cross-compiled information can be passed along to the magazine's advertisers.

And the names collected can be used by catalogs looking for a highly-targeted audience. What a lift over ''seat of the pants'' advertising!

Fax Machines

You already know how convenient fax machines have become. We see those blessed little inventions popping up everywhere. Once only in the office, they've found their way (as computers have) into many homes—and even cars. We use them as a quick and absolutely accurate way to enter a mail or catalog order.

A word of caution: It's easy to be seduced by new technologies and rely on a hot new razzle-dazzle medium to ''be'' the message as well as the means of conveying the message. The message becomes a technique without an idea.

The parallel should haunt any dedicated communicator. We've seen too many times how ineffective a communication becomes when it relies on mechanical trickery instead of decent salesmanship.

Don't forget: *Your* job is to match the message to the recipient. *Your medium's* job—whatever that medium may be—is to deliver the message, not create or replace it with gimmickry. Think of each new medium as another arrow in your quiver—and let psychology, not technology, be your tightly-strung bow.

So What Does All This Mean?

It means all parties to the marketing marriage should be aware of the strengths and weaknesses of the others.

If you're a conventional advertising writer looking for ways to make your message more effective, ask this question over and over as you write the ad: Am I motivating or just entertaining my reader?

If you're a direct marketer looking for ways to make your message more effective, ask this question over and over as you write the ad: Am I just writing a passionless description because I'm afraid to blend artistry with fact?

If you're forging new ad territories in the electronic age, ask this question over and over as you write the ad: Am I being seduced by new technology and forgetting to communicate?

> When you're your own most vociferous, critical, and effective critic . . . and you listen to the criticism. . . you're bound to be an effective communicator.

An Iconoclastic Quick Fix: Get Rid of Current Terminology

Iconoclastic though it may be, a suggestion: To speed up integration, let's eliminate the terms "direct" and "conventional." A marketer is a marketer. A communicator is a communicator.

Wait! First, let's be sure marketers and communicators do know the totality of marketing communication. Let's be sure every one of us in a decisionmaking posture knows the availability of every facet. . . and the benefit of integrating image and response.

For years advertisers have been satisfied if customers just remembered their ads. That's no longer good enough. One trend is unmistakable. Today's focus-group prime question isn't ''Did you remember the ad?'' but ''Did the ad convince you to act?''

In the 1990s, ''Awareness'' isn't enough.

Already, a genuine ''full-service'' advertising agency means a lot more than the ability to write and produce an ad and then buy print space, broadcast time, and printing. It means straddling every aspect of communications. Soon we'll no longer see direct response agencies...or advertising agencies...but strategic marketing communications agencies.

Obviously that includes direct marketing. In fact, it often means *emphasizing* direct marketing. We hear, ''Budgets are tight.'' We hear, ''Our ads aren't pulling.'' We hear, ''We have to figure out ways to sell more.''

All three statements could be translated to mean, ''We need an intelligent, powerful direct marketing addition to our campaign.''

Better yet, direct marketing isn't an addition. It isn't an appendage. It's the engine behind implementation of ''We need an integrated campaign if we're going to a) compete, b) maximize results, and c) build a cadre of repeat buyers.''

"Us," Not "We" and "They"

Let's accept as reality, not theory, what's going to happen. Image and response aren't going to inhabit separate universes.

The two components aren't going to be ''we'' and ''they.''

Practitioners of each aren't going to be able to snipe at each other. We can't say integration *will* happen because integration already *has* happened.

Late, but not too late.

The marriage of conventional advertising and direct marketing is *fact*. Depending on who you are, what you do, and whom you work for, it's a current fact or an about-to-be fact.

Direct marketing is no longer strictly tactical. Instead it's emerging as part of the overall marketing strategy: enhancement to an advertising message previously limited to image alone.

What We Have to Do

Our job as professional marketing communicators is to make our clients' business grow.

So an image ad needs to incorporate an element of response, a dialogue with the customer—enabling our company or our clients to sell more products or services. (Otherwise, in the competitive 1990s, we can be out of a job.)

And direct response advertising needs to incorporate the brand image—because the impression we leave with the non-responders is just as important as the response: Non-responders may respond another day if they remember favorably what we're selling.

What could be more logical?

INDEX

A

A/B split test, 39
Advertising Age, 1
Advertising executives ad, 127-28
Airline ads, 91-94, 134-35
American Demographics, 128-29, 143-44
Andiamo ads, 183-85
Announcement, 172
Announcement ad, 20-21
Apathy, 2
Artistic ads, 15-16
AT&T gold credit card ad, 186-88
Attention getting, 3
Authority, 158
Awards, 8, 199-200

B

Bifocals ad, 165-66
Bind-in card inserts, 68, 88-91, 93
Binding, selective, 99
Blind cash inducement ad, 112-113
Bon Appetit, 99
Boston College ads, 76-78
Bottled water promotion, 97-101
Bottle hanger ads, 100
Brochures, 71, 74, 76, 78
Budgets, 150-51
Bulk mail, 49
Burger King's ''Herb the Nerd''
    campaign, 7-8
Bus signboards, 100
Business market, 99
Business Marketing, 1-2

C

Car ads, 70-75
Card inserts, 68, 88-91, 93
Car phone ad, 33, 34

Catalog ads, 64-65, 94-95
Catalog copy, 130-34
Celebrity
    mail package, 55
    use of, 154
Chanel, Coco, 56
Checklist, 163-95
Chest-thumping, 189-90
Chevrolet ads, 70, 72-75
Chivas Regal ads, 9-12
Cigarette ads, 20-25
Citicorp, 204
Clio ad awards, 199
Coca-Cola, 49
Coffee ad, 89-91
Cointreau ad, 172-73
Comic book format, 58-59
Computer ads, 58-59, 86, 186-87
Computers, 201. *See also* Database,
    Electronic publishing.
Conde Nast Traveler, 149-50
Contest ad, 21-24
Conventional advertising, 3. *See also*
    General advertising.
Convincing copy, 25-26
Cooks, 99
Cookware contest, 84-85
Copywriters, *xiv*
Coupon, 91, 93, 160-61
    ad, 87-88
    dilemma, 84-89
    effectiveness test, 87
Creative strategy brief, 29-31
Creativity, 5
Credit card ads, 76-78, 186-88

D

Daily routine, *xiv*
Database, 21, 24
    interpretation of, 56, 60
    marketing, 203-4